NATHAN THE WISE

NATHAN THE WISE

DOVER THRIFT EDITIONS

Gotthold Ephraim Lessing

Translated from the German by
William Taylor

DOVER PUBLICATIONS, INC.
MINEOLA, NEW YORK

DOVER THRIFT EDITIONS

GENERAL EDITOR: MARY CAROLYN WALDREP
EDITOR OF THIS VOLUME: JANET B. KOPITO

Copyright

Theatrical Rights

This Dover Thrift Edition may be used in its entirety, in adaptation, or in any other way for theatrical productions, professional and amateur, in the United States, without permission, fee, or acknowledgment. (This may not apply outside of the United States, as copyright conditions may vary.)

Bibliographical Note

Nathan the Wise, first published by Dover Publications, Inc., in 2015, is an unabridged republication of the 1830 translation by William Taylor, published by Bernhard Tauchnitz, Leipzig, in 1868. A Note has been provided specially for this edition.

Library of Congress Cataloging-in-Publication Data

Lessing, Gotthold Ephraim, 1729–1781.
  Nathan der Weise. English
  Nathan the wise / Gotthold Ephraim Lessing ; translated by William Taylor.
    p. cm. — (Dover thrift editions)
  ISBN-13: 978-0-486-79676-5 (paperback)
  ISBN-10: 0-486-79676-0
    1. German drama. 2. Religious tolerance—Drama. I. Taylor,
  W. (William), 1765–1836, translator. II. Title.
  PT2403.A7T38 2015
  832'.6—dc23
                                                          2015003388

Manufactured in the United States by LSC Communications
79676006   2019
www.doverpublications.com

Note

The German dramatist and writer Gotthold Ephraim Lessing was born in Kamenz in 1729. Today he is seen as a figure of the Enlightenment era—a period coinciding with the Age of Reason and promoting religious tolerance and the questioning of institutionalized thinking. Lessing chose a literary career after studying medicine, philosophy, and theology. Drawn to Berlin, he showed a talent for writing and began reviewing the literature of the time, especially that of the theater. Because of his contribution to the Hamburg National Theatre, he came to be regarded as the first "dramaturge"—one who develops theatrical works through research, as well as creating the roster for a theatrical season, hiring performers, and editing the dramatic works themselves. In the 1760s, his dramatic works *Minna von Barnhelm* and *Hamburg Dramaturgy* were produced. Lessing also wrote an influential work of literary criticism, *Lacoon: An Essay on the Limits of Painting and Poetry* (1766). In 1776, he married Eva König. Sadly, they lost their infant son, and Eva died shortly after. Lessing died in 1781 after suffering a stroke.

Gotthold Lessing wrote what was to be his last work, *Nathan the Wise (Nathan der Weise)*, in 1779; it was first performed in 1783. Because its theme of religious tolerance antagonized the church, the play was not performed during Lessing's lifetime. Set during the Crusades, the drama examines the tensions among three religions—Judaism, Islam, and Christianity. The character Nathan draws from Lessing's friendship with the Jewish philosopher Moses Mendelssohn, also a notable figure of the Enlightenment, who encouraged respect for humankind's diverse religious beliefs.

Contents

Act I 1

Act II 23

Act III 44

Act IV 67

Act V 89

Nathan the Wise

DRAMATIS PERSONÆ

SALADIN, *the sultan.*

SITTAH, *his sister.*

NATHAN, *a rich jew.*

RECHA, *his adopted daughter.*

DAYA, *a christian woman dwelling with the jew as companion to Recha*

CONRADE, *a young templar.*

HAFI, *a dervis.*

ATHANASIOS, *the partriarch of Palestine.*

BONAFIDES, a friar.

An Emir, sundry Mamalukes, slaves, &c.

THE SCENE IS AT JERUSALEM.

NATHAN THE WISE.

Introite nam et heic Dii sunt!

Apud Gellium.

ACT I.

SCENE.—*A Hall in Nathan's House.*

NATHAN, *in a travelling dress,* DAYA *meeting him.*

DAYA. 'Tis he, 'tis Nathan! Thanks to the Almighty,
That you're at last return'd.
    NATHAN.   Yes, Daya, thanks,
That I have reach'd Jerusalem in safety.
But wherefore this *at last?* Did I intend,
Or was it possible to come back sooner?
As I was forc'd to travel, out and in,
'Tis a long hundred leagues to Babylon;
And to get in one's debts is no employment,
That speeds a traveller.
    DAYA.   O Nathan, Nathan,
How miserable you had nigh become
During this little absence; for your house—
    NATHAN. Well, 'twas on fire; I have already heard it.
God grant I may have heard the whole, that chanc'd!
    DAYA. 'Twas on the point of burning to the ground.
    NATHAN. Then we'd have built another, and a better.
    DAYA. True!—But thy Recha too was on the point
Of perishing amid the flames.

1

NATHAN.   Of perishing?
My Recha, saidst thou? She? I heard not that.
I then should not have needed any house.
Upon the point of perishing—perchance
She's gone?—Speak out then—out—torment me not
With this suspense.—Come, tell me—tell me all.
    DAYA. Were she no more, from me you would not hear it.
    NATHAN. Why then alarm me?—Recha, O my Recha!
    DAYA. Your Recha? Yours?
    NATHAN.   What if I ever were
Doom'd to unlearn to call this child, *my* child.
    DAYA. Is all you own yours by an equal title?
    NATHAN. Nought by a better. What I else enjoy
Nature and Fortune gave—this treasure, Virtue.
    DAYA. How dear you make me pay for all your goodness!—
If goodness, exercis'd with such a view,
Deserves the name.—
    NATHAN.   With such a view? With what?
    DAYA. My conscience—
    NATHAN.   Daya, let me tell you first—
    DAYA. I say, my conscience—
    NATHAN.   What a charming silk
I bought for you in Babylon! 'Tis rich,
Yet elegantly rich. I almost doubt
If I have brought a prettier for Recha.
    DAYA. And what of that.—I tell you that my conscience
Will not be longer hush'd.
    NATHAN.   And I have bracelets,
And ear-rings, and a neck-lace, which will charm you.
I chose them at Damascus.
    DAYA.   That's your way:—
If you can but make presents—but make presents.—
    NATHAN. Take you as freely as I give—and cease.
    DAYA. And cease?—Who questions, Nathan, but that you are
Honor and generosity in person;—
Yet—
    NATHAN. Yet I'm but a Jew.—That was your meaning.
    DAYA. You better know what was my meaning, Nathan.
    NATHAN. Well, well, no more of this.
    DAYA.   I shall be silent;
But what of sinful in the eye of heaven

Springs out of it—not I, not I could help;
It falls upon thy head.
    NATHAN.   So let it, Daya.
Where is she then? What stays her?—Surely, surely,
You're not amusing me—And does she know
That I'm arrived?
    DAYA.   That you yourself must speak to.
Terror still vibrates in her every nerve.
Her fancy mingles fire with all she thinks of.
Asleep, her soul seems busy; but awake,
Absent: now less than brute, now more than angel.
    NATHAN. Poor thing! What are we mortals—
    DAYA.   As she lay
This morning sleeping, all at once she started
And cried: "list! list! there come my father's camels!"
And then she droop'd again upon her pillow
And I withdrew—when, lo! you really came.
Her thoughts have only been with you—and him.
    NATHAN. And *him?* What him?
    DAYA.   With him, who from the fire
Preserv'd her life.
    NATHAN.   Who was it? Where is he,
That sav'd my Recha for me?
    DAYA.   A young templar,
Brought hither captive a few days ago,
And pardon'd by the sultan.
    NATHAN.   How, a *templar*
Dismiss'd with life by Saladin. In truth,
Not a less miracle was to preserve her.
God!—God!—
    DAYA. Without this man, who risk'd afresh
The sultan's unexpected boon, we'd lost her.
    NATHAN. Where is he, Daya, where's this noble youth?
Do, lead me to his feet. Sure, sure you gave him
What treasures I had left you—gave him all,
Promis'd him more—much more?
    DAYA.   How could we?
    NATHAN.   Not?
    DAYA. He came, he went, we know not whence, or whither.
Quite unacquainted with the house, unguided
But by his ear, he prest through smoke and flame,

His mantle spread before him, to the room
Whence pierc'd the shrieks for help; and we began
To think him lost—and her; when, all at once,
Bursting from flame and smoke, he stood before us,
She in his arm upheld. Cold and unmov'd
By our loud warmth of thanks, he left his booty,
Struggled into the crowd, and disappear'd.

    NATHAN. But not for ever, Daya, I would hope.

    DAYA. For some days after, underneath yon palms,
That shade his grave who rose again from death,
We saw him wandering up and down. I went,
With transport went to thank him. I conjur'd,
Intreated him to visit once again
The dear sweet girl he sav'd, who long'd to shed
At her preserver's feet the grateful tear—

    NATHAN. Well!

    DAYA.   But in vain. Deaf to our warmest prayers,
On me he flung such bitter mockery—

    NATHAN. That hence rebuff'd—

    DAYA.   Oh no, oh no, indeed not.
Daily I forc'd myself upon him, daily
Afresh encounter'd his dry taunting speeches.
Much I have borne, and would have borne much more:
But he of late forbears his lonely walk
Under the scatter'd palms, which stand about
Our holy sepulchre: nor have I learnt
Where he now is. You seem astonish'd—thoughtful—

    NATHAN. I was imagining what strange impressions
This conduct makes on such a mind as Recha's.
Disdain'd by one, whom she must feel compell'd
To venerate and to esteem so highly.
At once attracted and repell'd—the combat
Between her head and heart must yet endure,
Regret, Resentment, in unusual struggle.
Neither, perhaps, obtains the upper hand,
And busy Fancy, meddling in the fray,
Weaves wild enthusiasms to her dazzled spirit,
Now clothing Passion in the garb of Reason,
And Reason now in Passion's—do I err?
This last is Recha's fate.—Romantic notions—

    DAYA. Aye; but such pious, lovely, sweet, illusions.

NATHAN. Illusions tho'.

DAYA.   Yes: and the one, her bosom
Clings to most fondly, is, that the brave templar
Was but a transient inmate of the earth,
A guardian angel, such as from her childhood
She lov'd to fancy kindly hovering round her,
Who from his veiling cloud amid the fire
Stepp'd forth in her preserver's form. You smile—
Who knows? At least beware of banishing
So pleasing an illusion—if deceitful
Christian, Jew, Mussulman, agree to own it,
And 'tis—at least to her—a dear illusion.

NATHAN. Also to me. Go, my good Daya, go,
See what she's after. Can't I speak with her?
Then I'll find out our untam'd guardian angel,
Bring him to sojourn here awhile among us—
We'll pinion his wild wing, when once he's taken.

DAYA. You undertake too much.

NATHAN.   And when, my Daya,
This sweet illusion yields to sweeter truth,
(For to a man a man is ever dearer
Than any angel) you must not be angry
To see our lov'd enthusiast exorcis'd.

DAYA. You are so good—and yet so sly. I'll seek her,
But listen,—yes! she's coming of herself.

NATHAN, DAYA, *and* RECHA.

RECHA. And you are here, your very self, my father,
I thought you'd only sent your voice before you.
Where are you then? What mountains, deserts, torrents,
Divide us now? You see me, face to face,
And do not hasten to embrace your Recha.
Poor Recha! she was almost burnt alive,
But only—only—almost. Do not shudder!
O 'tis a horrid end to die in fire!

NATHAN *(embracing her).* My child, my darling child!

RECHA.   You had to cross
The Jordan, Tigris, and Euphrates, and
Who knows what rivers else. I us'd to tremble
And quake for you, till the fire came so nigh me;
Since then, methinks 'twere comfort, balm, refreshment,

To die by water. But you are not drown'd—
I am not burnt alive.—We will rejoice—
We will praise God—the kind good God, who bore thee,
Upon the buoyant wings of *unseen* angels,
Across the treacherous stream—the God, who bade
My angel *visibly* on his white wing
Athwart the roaring flame—

    NATHAN *(aside)*.   White wing?—oh aye
The broad white fluttering mantle of the templar.

    RECHA. Yes, visibly he bore me thro' the fire,
O'ershadow'd by his pinions.—Face to face
I've seen an angel, father, my own angel.

    NATHAN. Recha deserves it, and would see in him
No fairer form than he beheld in her.

    RECHA. Whom are you flattering, father—tell me now—
The angel, or yourself?

    NATHAN.   Yet had a man,
A man of those whom Nature daily fashions,
Done you this service, he to you had seem'd,
Had been an angel.

    RECHA.   No, not such a one.
Indeed it was a true and real angel.
And have not you yourself instructed me
How possible it is there may be angels;
That God for those who love him can work miracles—
And I do love him father—

    NATHAN.   And he thee;
And both for thee, and all like thee, my child,
Works daily wonders, from eternity
Has wrought them for you.

    RECHA.   That I like to hear.

    NATHAN. Well, and altho' it sounds quite natural,
An every day event, a simple story,
That you was by a real templar sav'd,
Is it the less a miracle? The greatest
Of all is this, that true and real wonders
Should happen so perpetually, so daily.
Without this universal miracle
A thinking man had scarcely call'd those such,
Which only children, Recha, ought to name so,
Who love to gape and stare at the unusual

And hunt for novelty—

DAYA.   Why will you then
With such vain subtleties, confuse her brain
Already overheated?

NATHAN.   Let me manage.—
And is it not enough then for my Recha
To owe her preservation to a man,
Whom no small miracle preserv'd himself.
For who e'er heard before that Saladin
Let go a templar; that a templar wish'd it,
Hop'd it, or for his ransom offer'd more
Than taunts, his leathern sword-belt, or his dagger?

RECHA. That makes for me: these are so many reasons
He was no real knight, but only seem'd it.
If in Jerusalem no captive templar,
Appears alive, or freely wanders round,
How could I find one, in the night, to save me?

NATHAN. Ingenious! dextrous! Daya, come in aid.
It was from you I learnt he was a prisoner;
Doubtless you know still more about him, speak.

DAYA. 'Tis but report indeed, but it is said
That Saladin bestow'd upon this youth
His gracious pardon for the strong resemblance
He bore a favourite brother—dead, I think
These twenty years—his name, I know it not—
He fell, I don't know where—and all the story
Sounds so incredible, that very likely
The whole is mere invention, talk, romance.

NATHAN. And why incredible? Would you reject
This story, tho' indeed it's often done,
To fix on something more incredible,
And give that faith? Why should not Saladin,
Who loves so singularly all his kindred,
Have lov'd in early youth with warmer fondness
A brother now no more. Do we not see
Faces alike, and is an old impression
Therefore a lost one? Do resembling features
Not call up like emotions. Where's th' incredible?
Surely, sage Daya, this can be to thee
No miracle, or do *thy* wonders only
Demand—I should have said *deserve* belief?

DAYA. You're on the bite.

NATHAN.   Were you quite fair with me?
Yet even so, my Recha, thy escape
Remains a wonder, only possible
To Him, who of the proud pursuits of princes
Makes sport—or if not sport—at least delights
To lead and manage them by slender threads.

RECHA. If I do err, it is not wilfully,
My father.

NATHAN.   No, you have been always docile.
See now, a forehead vaulted thus, or thus—
A nose bow'd one way rather than another—
Eye-brows with straiter, or with sharper curve—
A line, a mole, a wrinkle, a mere nothing
I' th' countenance of an European savage—
And thou—art sav'd, in Asia, from the fire.
Ask ye for signs and wonders after that?
What need of calling angels into play?

DAYA. But, Nathan, where's the harm, if I may speak,
Of fancying one's self by an angel sav'd,
Rather than by a man? Methinks it brings us
Just so much the nearer the incomprehensive
First cause of preservation.

NATHAN.   Pride, rank pride!
The iron pot would with a silver prong
Be lifted from the furnace—to imagine
Itself a silver vase. Psha! Where's the harm?
Thou askest. Where's the good? I might reply.
For thy *it brings us nearer to the Godhead*
Is nonsense, Daya, if not blasphemy.
But it does harm: yes, yes, it does indeed.
Attend now. To the being, who preserv'd you,
Be he an angel or a man, you both,
And thou especially wouldst gladly show
Substantial services in just requital.
Now to an angel what great services
Have ye the power to do? To sing his praise—
Melt in transporting contemplation o'er him—
Fast on his holiday—and squander alms—
What nothingness of use! To me at least
It seems your neighbour gains much more than he

By all this pious glow. Not by your fasting
Is he made fat; not by your squandering, rich;
Nor by your transports is his glory exalted;
Nor by your faith, his might. But to a man—
    DAYA. Why yes; a man indeed had furnish'd us
With more occasions to be useful to him.
God knows how readily we should have seiz'd them.
But then he would have nothing—wanted nothing—
Was in himself wrapt up, and self-sufficient,
As angels are.
    RECHA. And, when at last he vanish'd—
    NATHAN. Vanish'd? How vanish'd? Underneath the palms
Escap'd your view, and has return'd no more.
Or have you really sought for him elsewhere?
    DAYA. No, that indeed we've not.
    NATHAN.   Not, Daya, not?
See it does harm, hard-hearted, cold enthusiasts,
What if this angel on a bed of illness—
    RECHA. Illness?
    DAYA.   Ill! sure he is not.
    RECHA.   A cold shudder
Creeps over me; O Daya, feel my forehead,
It was so warm, 'tis now as chill as ice.
    NATHAN. He is a Frank, unus'd to this hot climate,
Is young, and to the labors of his calling,
To fasting, watching, quite unus'd—
    RECHA.   Ill—ill!
    DAYA. Thy father only means 'twere possible.
    NATHAN. And there he lies without a friend, or money
To buy him friends—
    RECHA.   Alas! my father.
    NATHAN.   Lies
Without advice, attendance, converse, pity,
The prey of agony, of death—
    RECHA.   Where—where?
    NATHAN. He, who, for one he never knew, or saw—
It is enough for him he is a man—
Plung'd into fire.
    DAYA.   O Nathan, Nathan, spare her.
    NATHAN. Who car'd not to know ought of her he sav'd,
Declin'd her presence to escape her thanks—

DAYA. Do, spare her!

NATHAN.   Did not wish to see her more,
Unless it were a second time to save her—
Enough for him he is a man—

DAYA.   Stop, look!

NATHAN. He—he, in death, has nothing to console him,
But the remembrance of this deed.

DAYA.   You kill her!

NATHAN. And you kill him—or might have done at least—
Recha 'tis medicine I give, not poison.
He lives—come to thyself—may not be ill—
Not even ill—

RECHA.   Surely not dead, not dead.

NATHAN. Dead surely not—for God rewards the good
Done here below, here too. Go; but remember
How easier far devout enthusiasm is
Than a good action; and how willingly
Our indolence takes up with pious rapture,
Tho' at the time unconscious of its end,
Only to save the toil of useful deeds.

RECHA. Oh never leave again thy child alone!—
But can he not be only gone a journey?

NATHAN. Yes, very likely. There's a mussulman
Numbering with curious eye my laden camels,
Do you know who he is?

DAYA.   Oh, your old dervis.

NATHAN. Who—who?

DAYA. Your chess-companion.

NATHAN.   That, Al-Hafi?

DAYA. And now the treasurer of Saladin.

NATHAN. Al-Hafi? Are you dreaming? How was this?
In fact it is so. He seems coming hither.
In with you quick.—What now am I to hear?

NATHAN and HAFI.

HAFI. Aye, lift thine eyes, and wonder.

NATHAN.   Is it you?
A dervis so magnificent!—

HAFI.   Why not?
Can nothing then be made out of a dervis?

NATHAN. Yes, surely; but I have been wont to think

A dervis, that's to say a thoro' dervis,
Will allow nothing to be made of him.
    HAFI. May-be 'tis true that I'm no thoro' dervis;
But, by the prophet, when we must—
    NATHAN.   Must, Hafi?
Needs must—belongs to no man: and a dervis—
    HAFI. When he is much besought, and thinks it right,
A dervis must.
    NATHAN.   Well spoken, by our God!
Embrace me, man, you're still, I trust, my friend.
    HAFI. Why not ask first what has been made of me?
    NATHAN. Ask climbers to look back!
    HAFI.   And may I not
Have grown to such a creature in the state
That my old friendship is no longer welcome?
    NATHAN. If you still bear your dervis-heart about you
I'll run the risk of that. Th' official robe
Is but your cloak.
    HAFI.   A cloak, that claims some honor.
What think'st thou? At a court of thine, how great
Had been Al-Hafi?
    NATHAN.   Nothing but a dervis.
If more, perhaps—what shall I say—my cook.
    HAFI. In order to unlearn my native trade.
Thy cook—why not thy butler too? The sultan,
He knows me better, I'm his treasurer.
    NATHAN. You, you?
    HAFI.   Mistake not—of the lesser purse—
His father manages the greater still—
The purser of his household.
    NATHAN.   That's not small.
    HAFI. 'Tis larger than thou think'st; for every beggar
Is of his household.
    NATHAN.   He's so much their foe—
    HAFI. That he'd fain root them out—with food and raiment—
Tho' he turn beggar in the enterprize.
    NATHAN. Bravo, I meant so.
    HAFI.   And he's almost such.
His treasury is every day, ere sun-set,
Poorer than empty; and how high so e'er
Flows in the morning tide, 'tis ebb by noon.

NATHAN. Because it circulates thro' such canals
As can be neither stopp'd, nor fill'd.
    HAFI.   Thou hast it.
    NATHAN. I know it well.
    HAFI.   Nathan, 'tis woeful doing
When kings are vultures amid carcases:
But when they're carcases amid the vultures
'Tis ten times worse.
    NATHAN.   No, dervis, no, no, no.
    HAFI. Thou mayst well talk so. Now then, let me hear
What wouldst thou give me to resign my office?
    NATHAN. What does it bring you in?
    HAFI.   To me, not much;
But thee, it might indeed enrich: for when,
As often happens, money is at ebb,
Thou couldst unlock thy sluices, make advances,
And take in form of interest all thou wilt.
    NATHAN. And interest upon interest of the interest—
    HAFI. Certainly.
    NATHAN.   Till my capital becomes
All interest.
    HAFI.   How—that does not take with thee?
Then write a finis to our book of friendship;
For I have reckon'd on thee.
    NATHAN.   How so, Hafi?
    HAFI. That thou wouldst help me to go thro' my office
With credit, grant me open chest with thee—
Dost shake thy head?
    NATHAN.   Let's understand each other.
Here's a distinction to be made. To you,
To dervis Hafi, all I have is open;
But to the defterdar of Saladin,
To that Al-Hafi—
    HAFI.   Spoken like thyself!
Thou hast been ever no less kind than cautious.
The two Al-Hafis thou distinguishest
Shall soon be parted. See this coat of honor,
Which Saladin bestow'd—before 'tis worn
To rags, and suited to a dervis' back,—
Will in Jerusalem hang upon the hook;
While I along the Ganges scorching strand,

Amid my teachers shall be wandering barefoot.

    NATHAN. That's like you.

    HAFI.   Or be playing chess among them.

    NATHAN. Your sovereign good.

    HAFI.   What dost thou think seduc'd me?

The wish of having not to beg in future—

The pride of acting the rich man to beggars—

Would these have metamorphos'd a rich beggar

So suddenly into a poor rich man?

    NATHAN. No, I think not.

    HAFI.   A sillier, sillier weakness.

For the first time my vanity was tempter,

Flatter'd by Saladin's good-hearted notion—

    NATHAN. Which was?

    HAFI.   That all a beggar's wants are only

Known to a beggar: such alone can tell

How to relieve them usefully and wisely.

"Thy predecessor was too cold for me,

"(He said) and when he gave, he gave unkindly;

"Informed himself with too precautious strictness

"Concerning the receiver, not content

"To learn the want, unless he knew its cause,

"And measuring out by that his niggard bounty.

"Thou wilt not thus bestow. So harshly kind

"Shall Saladin not seem in thee. Thou art not

"Like the choak'd pipe, whence sullied and by spurts

"Flow the pure waters it absorbs in silence.

"Al-Hafi thinks and feels like me." So nicely

The fowler whistled, that at last the quail

Ran to his net. Cheated, and by a cheat—

    NATHAN. Tush! dervis, gently.

    HAFI.   What! and is't not cheating,

Thus to oppress mankind by hundred thousands,

To squeeze, grind, plunder, butcher, and torment,

And act philanthropy to individuals?—

Not cheating—thus to ape from the Most High,

The bounty, which alike on mead and desert,

Upon the just and the unrighteous, falls

In sunshine or in showers, and not possess

The never empty hand of the Most High?—

Not cheating—

NATHAN. Cease!
HAFI.   Of my own cheating sure
It is allow'd to speak. Were it not cheating
To look for the fair side of these impostures,
In order, under color of its fairness,
To gain advantage from them—ha?
NATHAN.   Al-Hafi,
Go to your desert quickly. Among men
I fear you'll soon unlearn to be a man.
HAFI. And so do I—farewell.
NATHAN.   What, so abruptly?
Stay, stay, Al-Hafi; has the desert wings?
Man, 'twill not run away, I warrant you—
Hear, hear, I want you—want to talk with you—
He's gone. I could have liked to question him
About our templar. He will likely know him.

NATHAN *and* DAYA.

DAYA *(bursting in)*. O Nathan, Nathan!
NATHAN.   Well, what now?
DAYA.   He's there.
He shows himself again.
NATHAN. Who, Daya, who?
DAYA. He! he!
NATHAN.   When cannot He be seen? Indeed
Your He is only one; that should not be,
Were he an angel even.
DAYA.   'Neath the palms
He wanders up and down, and gathers dates.
NATHAN. And eats?—and as a templar?
DAYA.   How you tease us!
Her eager eye espy'd him long ago,
While he scarce gleam'd between the farther stems,
And follows him most punctually. Go,
She begs, conjures you, go without delay;
And from the window will make signs to you
Which way his rovings bend. Do, do make haste.
NATHAN. What thus, as I alighted from my camel,
Would that be decent? Swift, do you accost him,
Tell him of my return. I do not doubt,
His delicacy, in the master's absence,

Forbore my house; but gladly will accept
The father's invitation. Say, I ask him,
Most heartily request him—
    DAYA.   All in vain!
In short he will not visit any jew.
    NATHAN. Then do thy best endeavours to detain him,
Or with thine eyes to watch his further haunt,
Till I rejoin you. I shall not be long.

SCENE.—*A Place of Palms.*

The TEMPLAR *walking to and fro, a* FRIAR *following him at some
distance, as if desirous of addressing him.*

    TEMPLAR. This fellow does not follow me for pastime.
How skaunt he eyes his hands! Well, my good brother,
Perhaps I should say, father; ought I not?
    FRIAR. No—brother—a lay-brother at your service.
    TEMPLAR. Well, brother, then; if I myself had something—
But—but, by God, I've nothing.
    FRIAR.   Thanks the same;
And God reward your purpose thousand-fold!
The will, and not the deed, makes up the giver.
Nor was I sent to follow you for alms—
    TEMPLAR. Sent then?
    FRIAR.   Yes, from the monastery.
    TEMPLAR.   Where
I was just now in hopes of coming in
For pilgrims' fare.
    FRIAR.   They were already at table:
But if it suit with you to turn directly—
    TEMPLAR. Why so? 'tis true, I have not tasted meat
This long time. What of that? The dates are ripe.
    FRIAR. O with that fruit go cautiously to work.
Too much of it is hurtful, sours the humors,
Makes the blood melancholy.
    TEMPLAR.   And if I
Choose to be melancholy—For this warning
You were not sent to follow me, I ween.
    FRIAR. Oh no: I only was to ask about you,
And feel your pulse a little.

TEMPLAR.   And you tell me
Of that yourself?
    FRIAR. Why not?
    TEMPLAR.   A deep one! troth:
And has your cloister more such?
    FRIAR.   I can't say.
Obedience is our bounden duty.
    TEMPLAR.   So—
And you obey without much scrupulous questioning?
    FRIAR. Were it obedience else, good Sir?
    TEMPLAR.   How is it
The simple mind is ever in the right.
May you inform me, who it is, that wishes
To know more of me? 'Tis not you yourself,
I dare be sworn.
    FRIAR.   Would it become me, Sir,
Or benefit me?
    TEMPLAR.   Whom can it become,
Whom can it benefit, to be so curious?
    FRIAR. The patriarch I presume—'twas he that sent me.
    TEMPLAR. The patriarch? Knows he not my badge, the cross
Of red on the white mantle?
    FRIAR.   Can I say?
    TEMPLAR. Well, brother, well; I am a templar, taken
Prisoner at Tebnin, whose exalted fortress,
Just as the truce expir'd, we sought to climb,
In order to push forward next to Sidon.
I was the twentieth captive, but the only
Pardon'd by Saladin—with this, the patriarch
Knows all, or more, than his occasions ask.
    FRIAR. And yet no more than he already knows,
I think. But why alone of all the captives
Thou hast been spar'd, he fain would learn—
    TEMPLAR.   Can I
Myself tell that? Already, with bare neck,
I kneel'd upon my mantle, and awaited
The blow; when Saladin, with steadfast eye
Fix'd me, sprang nearer to me, made a sign—
I was uprais'd, unbound, about to thank him,—
And saw his eye in tears. Both stand in silence.
He goes. I stay. How all this hangs together,

Thy patriarch may unriddle.

FRIAR.   He concludes,

That God preserv'd you for some mighty deed.

 TEMPLAR. Some mighty deed? To save out of the fire
A jewish girl—to usher curious pilgrims
About mount Sinai—to—

 FRIAR.   The time may come—

And this is no such trifle—but perhaps
The patriarch meditates a weightier office.

 TEMPLAR. Think you so, brother, has he hinted ought?

 FRIAR. Why yes; I was to sift you out a little,
And hear if you were one to—

 TEMPLAR.   Well—to what?

I'm curious to observe how this man sifts.

 FRIAR. The shortest way will be to tell you plainly
What are the patriarch's wishes.

 TEMPLAR. And they are—

 FRIAR. To send a letter by your hand.

 TEMPLAR.   By me?

I am no carrier. And were that an office
More meritorious than to save from burning
A jewish maid?

 FRIAR. So it should seem; must seem—

For, says the patriarch, to all Christendom
This letter is of import:—and to bear it
Safe to its destination, says the patriarch,
God will reward with a peculiar crown
In heaven:—and of this crown, the patriarch says,
No one is worthier than you:—

 TEMPLAR.   Than I?

 FRIAR. For none so able, and so fit to earn
This crown, the patriarch says, as you.

 TEMPLAR.   As I?

 FRIAR. The patriarch here is free, can look about him,
And knows, he says, how cities may be storm'd,
And how defended; knows, he says, the strengths
And weaknesses of Saladin's new bulwark,
And of the inner rampart last thrown up;
And to the warriors of the Lord, he says,
Could clearly point them out;—

 TEMPLAR.   And can I know

Exactly the contents of this same letter?

 FRIAR. Why that I don't pretend to vouch exactly—
'Tis to king Philip: and our patriarch—
I often wonder how this holy man,
Who lives so wholly to his God and heaven,
Can stoop to be so well inform'd about
Whatever passes here—'Tis a hard task!

 TEMPLAR. Well—and your patriarch—

 FRIAR.   Knows, with great precision,
And from sure hands, how, when, and with what force,
And in which quarter, Saladin, in case
The war breaks out afresh, will take the field.

 TEMPLAR. He knows that?

 FRIAR.   Yes; and would acquaint king Philip,
That he may better calculate, if really
The danger be so great as to require
Him to renew at all events the truce
So bravely broken by your body.

 TEMPLAR.   So?
This is a patriarch indeed! He wants
No common messenger; he wants a spy.
Go tell your patriarch, brother, I am not,
As far as you can sift, the man to suit him.
I still esteem myself a prisoner, and
A templar's only calling is to fight,
And not to ferret out intelligence.

 FRIAR. That's much as I suppos'd, and, to speak plainly,
Not to be blam'd. The best is yet behind.
The patriarch has made out the very fortress,
Its name, and strength, and site on Libanon,
Wherein the mighty sums are now conceal'd,
With which the prudent father of the sultan
Provides the cost of war, and pays the army.
He knows that Saladin, from time to time,
Goes to this fortress, thro' by-ways and passes,
With few attendants.

 TEMPLAR.   Well—

 FRIAR.   How easy 'twere
To seize his person in these expeditions,
And make an end of all! You shudder, Sir—
Two Maronites, who fear the Lord, have offer'd

Nathan the Wise

To share the danger of the enterprize,
Under a proper leader.
   TEMPLAR.   And the patriarch
Had cast his eye on me for this brave office?
   FRIAR. He thinks king Philip might from Ptolemais
Best second such a deed.
   TEMPLAR.   On me? on me?
Have you not heard then, just now heard, the favor,
Which I receiv'd from Saladin?
   FRIAR.   O yes!
   TEMPLAR. And yet?
   FRIAR.   The patriarch thinks—that's mighty well—
God, and the order's interest—
   TEMPLAR.   Alter nothing,
Command no villainies.
   FRIAR.   No, that indeed not;
But what is villainy in human eyes
May in the sight of God, the patriarch thinks,
Not be—
   TEMPLAR.   I owe my life to Saladin,
And might take his?
   FRIAR.   That—fie! But Saladin,
The patriarch thinks, is yet the common foe
Of Christendom, and cannot earn a right
To be your friend.
   TEMPLAR.   My friend—because I will not
Behave, like an ungrateful scoundrel to him.
   FRIAR. Yet gratitude, the patriarch thinks, is not
A debt, before the eye of God, or man,
Unless for our own sakes the benefit
Had been conferred; and, it has been reported,
The patriarch understands, that Saladin
Preserv'd your life, merely because your voice,
Your air, or features, rais'd a recollection
Of his lost brother.
   TEMPLAR.   He knows this? and yet—
If it were sure, I should—ah Saladin!
How! and shall nature then have form'd in me
A single feature in thy brother's likeness,
With nothing in my soul to answer to it?
Or what does correspond shall I suppress

To please a patriarch? So thou dost not cheat us,
Nature—and so not contradict thyself,
Kind God of all.—Go, brother, go away:
Do not stir up my anger.

    FRIAR.   I withdraw
More gladly than I came. We cloister-folk
Are forc'd to vow obedience to superiors.
                                      [*Goes.*

TEMPLAR *and* DAYA.

    DAYA. The monk methinks left him in no good mood:
But I must risk my message.
    TEMPLAR.   Better still!
The proverb says: that monks and women are
The devil's clutches; and I'm tost to–day
From one to th' other.
    DAYA.   Whom do I behold?—
Thank God! I see you, noble knight, once more.
Where have you lurk'd this long, long space? You've not
Been ill?
    TEMPLAR.   No.
    DAYA. Well, then?
    TEMPLAR. Yes.
    DAYA.   We've all been anxious,
Lest something ail'd you.
    TEMPLAR.   So?
    DAYA.   Have you been journeying?
    TEMPLAR. Hit off!
    DAYA.   How long return'd?
    TEMPLAR.   Since yesterday.
    DAYA. Our Recha's father too is just return'd,
And now may Recha hope at last—
    TEMPLAR.   For what?
    DAYA. For what she often has requested of you.
Her father pressingly invites your visit.
He now arrives from Babylon, with twenty
High-laden camels, brings the curious drugs,
And precious stones, and stuffs, he has collected
From Syria, Persia, India, even China.
    TEMPLAR. I am no chap.
    DAYA.   His nation honors him,

As if he were a prince, and yet to hear him
Call'd the *wise* Nathan by them, not the *rich*,
Has often made me wonder.

TEMPLAR.   To his nation
Are *rich* and *wise* perhaps of equal import.

DAYA. But above all he should be call'd the *good*.
You can't imagine how much goodness dwells
Within him. Since he has been told the service
You render'd to his Recha, there is nothing
That he would grudge you.

TEMPLAR.   Aye?

DAYA.   Do, see him, try him.

TEMPLAR. A burst of feeling soon is at an end.

DAYA. And do you think that I, were he less kind,
Less bountiful, had hous'd with him so long:
That I don't feel my value as a christian:
For 'twas not o'er my cradle said, or sung,
That I to Palestina should pursue
My husband's steps, only to educate
A jewess. My husband was a noble page
In emperor Frederic's army.

TEMPLAR.   And by birth
A Switzer, who obtain'd the gracious honor
Of drowning in one river with his master.
Woman how often you have told me this!
Will you ne'er leave off persecuting me?

DAYA. My Jesus! persecute—

TEMPLAR.   Aye, persecute.
Observe then, I henceforward will not see,
Not hear you, nor be minded of a deed
Over and over, which I did unthinking,
And which, when thought about, I wonder at.
I wish not to repent it; but, remember,
Should the like accident occur again,
'Twill be your fault if I proceed more coolly,
Ask a few questions, and let burn what's burning.

DAYA. My God forbid!

TEMPLAR.   From this day forth, good woman,
Do me at least the favor not to know me:
I beg it of you: and don't send the father.
A jew's a jew, and I am rude, and bearish.

The image of the maid is quite erased
Out of my soul—if it was ever there—

DAYA. But your's remains with her.

TEMPLAR.　　　　　Why so—what then—

Wherefore give harbour to it?—

DAYA.　　　　　Who knows wherefore?

Men are not always what they seem to be.

TEMPLAR. They're seldom better than they seem to be.

DAYA. Ben't in this hurry.

TEMPLAR.　　　　　Pray, forbear to make

These palm-trees odious. I have lov'd to walk here.

DAYA. Farewell then, bear. Yet I must track the savage.

ACT II.

SCENE.—*The Sultan's Palace.—An outer-room of Sittah's apartment.*

SALADIN *and* SITTAH, *playing chess.*

SITTAH. Wherefore so absent, brother? How you play!
SALADIN. Not well? I thought—
SITTAH.   Yes; very well for me.
Take back that move.
SALADIN. Why?
SITTAH.   Don't you see the knight
Becomes expos'd?
SALADIN. 'Tis true: then so.
SITTAH.   And so
I take the pawn.
SALADIN.   That's true again. Then, check!
SITTAH. That cannot help you. When my king is castled
All will be safe.
SALADIN.   But out of my dilemma
'Tis not so easy to escape unhurt.
Well, you must have the knight.
SITTAH.   I will not have him,
I pass him by.
SALADIN.   In that, there's no forbearance:
The place is better than the piece.
SITTAH.   May be.
SALADIN. Beware you reckon not without your host;
This stroke you did not think of.
SITTAH.   No indeed;
I did not think you tired of your queen.
SALADIN. My queen?

23

SITTAH. Well, well, I find that I to-day
Shall earn a thousand dinars to an asper.

    SALADIN. How so, my sister?

    SITTAH.   Play the ignorant—
As if it were not purposely thou losest.
I find not my account in 't; for, besides
That such a game yields very little pastime,
When have I not, by losing, won with thee?
When hast thou not, by way of comfort to me
For my lost game, presented twice the stake?

    SALADIN. So that it may have been on purpose, sister,
That thou hast lost at times.

    SITTAH.   At least, my brother's
Great liberality may be one cause
Why I improve no faster.

    SALADIN.   We forget
The game before us: let us make an end of it.

    SITTAH. I move—So—Now then—Check! and check again!

    SALADIN. This countercheck I wasn't aware of, Sittah,
My queen must fall the sacrifice.

    SITTAH.   Let's see—
Could it be help'd?

    SALADIN.   No, no, take off the queen!
That is a piece, which never thrives with me.

    SITTAH. Only that piece?

    SALADIN.   Off with it! I shan't miss it.
Thus I guard all again.

    SITTAH.   How civilly
We should behave to queens, my brother's lessons
Have taught me but too well.

    SALADIN.   Take her, or not,
I stir the piece no more.

    SITTAH.   Why should I take her?
Check!

    SALADIN.   Go on.

    SITTAH.   Check!—

    SALADIN.   And check-mate?

    SITTAH.   Hold! not yet.
You may advance the knight, and ward the danger,
Or, as yon will—it is all one.

    SALADIN.   It is so.

You are the winner, and Al-Hafi pays.
Let him be call'd. Sittah, you was not wrong;
I seem to recollect I was unmindful—
A little absent. One isn't always willing
To dwell upon some shapeless bits of wood
Coupled with no idea. Yet the Imam,
When I play with him, bends with such abstraction.—
The loser seeks excuses. Sittah, 'twas not
The shapeless men, and the unmeaning squares,
That made me heedless—your dexterity,
Your calm sharp eye.

    SITTAH.   And what of that, good brother,
Is that to be th' excuse for your defeat?
Enough—you play'd more absently than I.

    SALADIN. Than you, what dwells upon your mind? my Sittah.
Not your own cares, I doubt—

    SITTAH.   O Saladin,
When shall we play again so constantly?

    SALADIN. An interruption will but whet our zeal.
You think of the campaign. Well, let it come.
It was not I, who first unsheath'd the sword.
I would have willingly prolong'd the truce,
And willingly have knit a closer bond,
A lasting one, have given to my Sittah
A husband worthy of her, Richard's brother.

    SITTAH. You love to talk of Richard.

    SALADIN.   Richard's sister
Might then have been allotted to our Melek.
O what a house that would have form'd—the first—
The best—and what is more— of earth the happiest!
You know I am not loath to praise myself;
Why should I— Of my friends am I not worthy?
O we had then led lives!

    SITTAH.   A pretty dream.
It makes me smile. You do not know the christians.
You will not know them. 'Tis this people's pride
Not to be men, but to be christians. Even
What of humane their founder felt, and taught,
And left to savour their fond superstition,
They value not because it is humane,
Lovely, and good for man; they only prize it

Because 'twas Christ who taught it, Christ who did it.
'Tis well for them he was so good a man:
Well that they take his goodness all for granted,
And in his virtues put their trust. His virtues—
'Tis not his virtues, but his name alone
They wish to trust upon us—'Tis his name
Which they desire should overspread the world,
Should swallow up the name of all good men,
And put the best to shame. 'Tis his mere name
They care for—

SALADIN.   Else, my Sittah, as thou sayst,
They would not have requir'd that thou, and Melek,
Should be called christians, ere you might be suffer'd,
To feel for christians conjugal affection.

SITTAH. As if from christians only, and as christians,
That love could be expected, which our maker
In man and woman for each other planted.

SALADIN. The christians do believe such idle notions,
They well might fancy this: and yet thou errest.
The templars, not the christians, are in fault.
'Tis not as christians, but as templars, that
They thwart my purpose. They alone prevent it.
They will on no account evacuate Acca,
Which was to be the dower of Richard's sister,
And, lest their order suffer, use this cant—
Bring into play the nonsense of the monk—
And scarcely would await the truce's end
To fall upon us. Go on so—go on,
To me you're welcome, Sirs. Would all things else
Went but as right!

SITTAH.   What else should trouble thee,
If this do not?

SALADIN.   Why that, which ever has.
I've been on Libanon, and seen our father.
He's full of care.

SITTAH.   Alas!

SALADIN.   He can't make shift,
Straiten'd on all sides, put off, disappointed;
Nothing comes in.

SITTAH. What fails him, Saladin?

SALADIN. What? but the thing I scarcely deign to name,

Which, when I have it, so superfluous seems,
And, when I have it not, so necessary.
Where is Al-Hafi then—this fatal money—
O welcome, Hafi!

HAFI, SALADIN, and SITTAH.

HAFI.   I suppose the gold
From Egypt is arriv'd.
 SALADIN.   Hast tidings of it?
 HAFI. I? no not I. I thought to have ta'en it here.
 SALADIN. To Sittah pay a thousand dinars.
 HAFI.   Pay?
And not receive—that's something less than nothing—
To Sittah and again to Sittah—and
Once more for loss at chess? Is this your game?
 SITTAH. Dost grudge me my good fortune?
 HAFI (examining the board).   Grudge! you know—
 SITTAH (making signs to Hafi). Hush, Hafi, hush!
 HAFI.   And were the white men yours?
You gave the check?
 SITTAH.   'Tis well he does not hear.
 HAFI. And he to move?
 SITTTAH. (approaching Hafi).   Say then aloud that I
Shall have my money.
 HAFI (still considering the game).   Yes, yes! you shall have it—
As you have always had it.
 SITTAH.   Are you crazy?
 HAFI. The game is not decided; Saladin,
You have not lost.
 SALADIN (scarcely hearkening).   Well, well—pay, pay.
 HAFI.   Pay, pay—
There stands your queen.
 SALADIN (still walking about).   It boots not, she is useless.
 SITTAH (low to Hafi). Do say that I may send and fetch the
gold.
 HAFI. Aye, aye, as usual—But altho' the queen
Be useless, you are by no means check-mate.
 SALADIN (dashes down the board). I am. I will then—
 HAFI.   So! small pains, small gains;
As got, so spent.
 SALADIN (to Sittah).   What is he muttering there?

SITTAH *(to Saladin, winking meanwhile to Hafi).* You know him
well, and his unyielding way.
He chooses to be pray'd to—may be he's envious—
  SALADIN. No not of thee, not of my sister, surely.
What do I hear, Al-Hafi, are you envious?
  HAFI. Perhaps. I'd rather have her head than mine,
Or her heart either.
  SITTAH.   Ne'ertheless, my brother,
He pays me right, and will again to-day.
Let him alone. There, go away Al-Hafi,
I'll send and fetch my dinars.
  HAFI.   No, I will not,
I will not act this farce a moment longer:
He shall, must know it.
  SALADIN.   Who? what?
  SITTAH.   O Al-Hafi,
Is this thy promise, this thy keeping word?
  HAFI. How could I think it was to go so far?
  SALADIN. Well, what am I to know?
  SITTAH.   I pray thee, Hafi,
Be more discreet.
  SALADIN.   That's very singular.
And what can Sittah then so earnestly,
So warmly have to sue for from a stranger,
A dervis, rather than from me, her brother?
Al-Hafi, I command. Dervis, speak out.
  SITTAH. Let not a trifle, brother, touch you nearer
Than is becoming. You know I have often
Won the same sum of you at chess, and, as
I have not just at present need of money,
I've left the sum at rest in Hafi's chest,
Which is not over full; and thus the stakes
Are not yet taken out—but, never fear,
It is not my intention to bestow them
On thee, or Hafi.
  HAFI. Were it only this—
  SITTAH. Some more such trifles are perhaps unclaim'd,
My own allowance, which you set apart,
Has lain some months untouch'd.
  HAFI.   Nor is that all—
  SALADIN. Nor yet—speak then!

HAFI.   Since we have been expecting
The treasure out of Egypt, she not only—
    SITTAH. Why listen to him?
    HAFI.   Has not had an asper;—
    SALADIN. Good creature—but, has been advancing to thee—
    HAFI. Has at her sole expense maintain'd thy state.
    SALADIN. *(embracing her).* My sister—ah!
    SITTAH.   And who but you, my brother,
Could make me rich enough to have the power?
    HAFI. And in a little time again will leave thee
Poor as himself.
    SALADIN.   I, poor—her brother, poor?
When had I more, when less than at this instant?
A cloak, a horse, a sabre, and a God!—
What need I else? With them what can be wanting?
And yet, Al-Hafi, I could quarrel with thee
For this.
    SITTAH.   A truce to that, my brother. Were it
As easy to remove our father's cares.
    SALADIN. Ah! now my joy thou hast at once abated;
To me there is, there can be, nothing wanting;
But, but to him—and, in him, to us all.
What shall I do? From Egypt may be nothing
Will come this long time. Why—God only knows.
We hear of no stir. To reduce, to spare,
I am quite willing for myself to stoop to,
Were it myself, and only I, should suffer—
But what can that avail? A cloak, a horse,
A sword, I ne'er can want;—as to my God,
He is not to be bought, he asks but little,
Only my heart. I had rely'd, Al-Hafi,
Upon a surplus in my chest.
    HAFI.   A surplus?
And tell me, would you not have had me impal'd
Or hang'd at least, if you had found me out
In hoarding up a surplus. Deficits,
Those one may venture on.
    SALADIN.   Well, but how next?
Could you have found out no one where to borrow
Unless of Sittah?
    SITTAH.   And would I have borne

To see the preference given to another?
I still lay claim to it. I am not as yet
Entirely bare.
    SALADIN.   Not yet entirely—This
Was wanting still. Go, turn thyself about;
Take where, and as, thou canst; be quick, Al-Hafi.
Borrow on promise, contract, any how;
But heed me—not of those I have enrich'd—
To borrow there might seem to ask it back.
Go to the covetous. They'll gladliest lend—
They know how well their money thrives with me—
    HAFI. I know none such.
    SITTAH.   I recollect just now
I heard Al-Hafi of thy friend's return.
    HAFI *(startled)*. Friend—friend of mine—and who should that be?
    SITTAH.   Who?
Thy vaunted jew!
    HAFI. A jew—and prais'd by me?
    SITTAH. To whom his God (I think I still retain
Thy own expression us'd concerning him)
To whom, of all the good things of this world,
His God in full abundance has bestow'd
The greatest and the least.
    HAFI.   What could I mean
When I said so?
    SITTAH.   The least of good things, riches;
The greatest, wisdom.
    HAFI.   How—and of a jew
Could I say that?
    SITTAH.   Didst thou not—of thy Nathan?
    HAFI. Hi ho! of him—of Nathan? At that moment
He did not come across me. But in fact,
He is at length come home; and, I suppose,
Is not ill off. His people us'd to call him
The wise—also the rich.
    SITTAH.   The rich, he's nam'd
Now more than ever. The whole town resounds
With news of jewels, costly stuffs, and stores,
That he brings back.
    HAFI.   Is he the rich again—
He'll be, no fear of it, once more the wise.

SITTAH. What thinkst thou, Hafi, of a call on him?

HAFI. On him—sure not to borrow—why, you know him—
He lend? Therein his very wisdom lies,
That he lends no one.

SITTAH.   Formerly thou gav'st
A very different picture of this Nathan.

HAFI. In case of need he'll lend you merchandize,
But money, money, never. He's a jew,
There are but few such! he has understanding,
Knows life, plays chess; but is in bad notorious
Above his brethren, as he is in good.
On him rely not. To the poor indeed
He vies perhaps with Saladin in giving:
Tho' he distributes less, he gives as freely,
As silently, as nobly, to jew, christian,
Mahometan, or parsee—'tis all one.

SITTAH. And such a man should be—

SALADIN.   How comes it then
I never heard of him?

SITTAH.   Should be unwilling
To lend to Saladin, who wants for others,
Not for himself?

HAFI.   Aye there peeps out the jew,
The ordinary jew. Believe me, prince,
He's jealous, really envious of your giving.
To earn God's favor seems his very business.
He lends not, that he may always have to give.
The law commandeth mercy, not compliance:
And thus for mercy's sake he's uncomplying.
'Tis true, I am not now on the best terms
With Nathan, but, I must entreat you, think not
That therefore I would do injustice to him.
He's good in every thing; but not in that—
Only in that. I'll knock at other doors.
I just have recollected an old moor,
Who's rich and covetous—I go—I go.

SITTAH. Why in such hurry, Hafi?

SALADIN.   Let him go.

SALADIN *and* SITTAH.

SITTAH. He hastens, like a man, who would escape me;

Why so? Was he indeed deceiv'd in Nathan,
Or does he play upon us?

    SALADIN.   Can I guess?
I scarcely know of whom you have been talking,
And hear to-day, for the first time, of Nathan.

    SITTAH. Is't possible the man were hid from thee,
Of whom, 'tis said, he has found out the tombs
Of Solomon and David, knows the word
That lifts their marble lids, and thence obtains
The golden oil and that feeds his shining pomp.

    SALADIN. Were this man's wealth by miracle created,
'Tis not at David's tomb, or Solomon's,
That 'twould be wrought. Not virtuous men lie there.

    SITTAH. His source of opulence is more productive,
And more exhaustless than a cave of Mammon.

    SALADIN. He trades, I hear.

    SITTAH.   His ships fill every harbour;
His caravans thro' every desert toil.
This has Al-Hafi told me long ago:
With transport adding then—how nobly Nathan
Bestows what he esteems it not a meanness
By prudent industry to have justly earn'd—
How free from prejudice his lofty soul—
His heart to every virtue how unlock'd—
With every lovely feeling how familiar.

    SALADIN. Yet Hafi spake just now so coldly of him.

    SITTAH. Not coldly; but with awkwardness, confusion,
As if he thought it dangerous to praise him,
And yet knew not to blame him undeserving.
Or can it really be that e'en the best
Among a people cannot quite escape
The tinges of the tribe; and that, in fact,
Al-Hafi has in this to blush for Nathan?
Be that as't may—be he the jew or no—
Is he but rich—that is enough for us.

    SALADIN. You would not, sister, take his wealth by force.

    SITTAH. What do you mean by force—fire, sword? O no!
What force is necessary with the weak
But their own weakness? Come awhile with me
Into my harem: I have bought a songstress,

You have not heard her, she came yesterday:
Meanwhile I'll think somewhat about a project
I have upon this Nathan. Follow, brother.

SCENE.—*The Place of Palms, close to Nathan's House.*

NATHAN, *attir'd, comes out with* RECHA.

RECHA. You have been so very slow, my dearest father,
You now will hardly be in time to find him.
    NATHAN. Well, if not here beneath the palms; yet, surely,
Elsewhere. My child, be satisfied. See, see,
Is not that Daya making towards us?
    RECHA. She certainly has lost him then.
    NATHAN.   Why so?
    RECHA. Else she'd walk quicker.
    NATHAN.   She may not have seen us.
    RECHA. There, now she sees us.
    NATHAN.   And her speed redoubles.
Be calm, my Recha.
    RECHA.   Would you have your daughter
Be cool and unconcern'd who 'twas that sav'd her,
Heed not to whom is due the life she prizes
Chiefly because she ow'd it first to thee?
    NATHAN. I would not wish thee other than thou art,
E'en if I knew that in they secret soul
A very different emotion throbs.
    RECHA. Why—what my father?
    NATHAN.   Dost thou ask of me,
So tremblingly of me, what passes in thee?
Whatever 'tis, 'tis innocence and nature.
Be not alarm'd, it gives me no alarm;
But promise me that, when thy heart shall speak
A plainer language, thou wilt not conceal
A single of thy wishes from my fondness.
    RECHA. O the mere possibility of wishing
Rather to veil and hide them makes me shudder.
    NATHAN. Let this be spoken once for all. Well Daya—

NATHAN, RECHA, *and* DAYA.

DAYA. He still is here beneath the palms, and soon
Will reach yon wall. See, there he comes.

RECHA.   And seems
Irresolute where next; if left or right.

DAYA. I know he mostly passes to the convent,
And therefore comes this path. What will you lay me?

RECHA. O yes he does. And did you speak to him?
How did he seem to-day?

DAYA.   As heretofore.

NATHAN. Don't let him see you with me: further back;
Or rather to the house.

RECHA.   Just one peep more.
Now the hedge steals him from me.

DAYA.   Come away.
Your father's in the right—should he perceive us,
'Tis very probable he'll tack about.

RECHA. But for the hedge—

NATHAN.   Now he emerges from it.
He can't but see you: hence—I ask it of you.

DAYA. I know a window whence we yet may—

RECHA.   Aye.

                    [*Goes in with Daya.*

NATHAN. I'm almost shy of this strange fellow, almost
Shrink back from his rough virtue. That one man
Should ever make another man feel awkward!
And yet—He's coming—ha!—by God, the youth
Looks like a man. I love his daring eye,
His open gait. May be the shell is bitter;
But not the kernel surely. I have seen
Some such, methinks. Forgive me, noble Frank.

NATHAN *and* TEMPLAR.

TEMPLAR. What?

NATHAN. Give me leave.

TEMPLAR. Well, jew, what wouldst thou have?

NATHAN. The liberty of speaking to you.

TEMPLAR.   So—
Can I prevent it? Quick then, what's your business?

NATHAN. Patience—nor hasten quite so proudly by
A man, who has not merited contempt,

And whom, for evermore, you've made your debtor.

TEMPLAR. How so? Perhaps I guess—No—Are you then—

NATHAN. My name is Nathan, father to the maid
Your generous courage snatch'd from circling flames,
And hasten—

TEMPLAR.   If with thanks, keep, keep them all.
Those little things I've had to suffer much from:
Too much already, far. And, after all,
You owe me nothing. Was I ever told
She was your daughter? 'Tis a templar's duty
To rush to the assistance of the first
Poor wight that needs him; and my life just then
Was quite a burden. I was mighty glad
To risk it for another; tho' it were
That of a jewess.

NATHAN.   Noble, and yet shocking!
The turn might be expected. Modest greatness
Wears willingly the mask of what is shocking
To scare off admiration: but, altho'
She may disdain the tribute, admiration,
Is there no other tribute she can bear with?
Knight, were you here not foreign, not a captive,
I would not ask so freely. Speak, command,
In what can I be useful?

TEMPLAR.   You—in nothing.

NATHAN. I'm rich.

TEMPLAR.   To me the richer jew ne'er seem'd
The better jew.

NATHAN.   Is that a reason why
You should not use the better part of him,
His wealth?

TEMPLAR.   Well, well, I'll not refuse it wholly,
For my poor mantle's sake—when that is threadbare,
And spite of darning will not hold together,
I'll come and borrow cloth, or money of thee,
To make me up a new one. Don't look solemn;
The danger is not pressing; 'tis not yet
At the last gasp, but tight and strong and good,
Save this poor corner, where an ugly spot
You see is singed upon it. It got singed
As I bore off your daughter from the fire.

NATHAN *(taking hold of the mantle)*. 'Tis singular that such
an ugly spot
Bears better testimony to the man,
Than his own mouth. This brand—O I could kiss it!
Your pardon—that I meant not.

TEMPLAR.   What?

NATHAN.   A tear
Fell on the spot.

TEMPLAR.   You'll find up more such tears—
(This jew methinks begins to work upon me).

NATHAN. Would you send once this mantle to my daughter?

TEMPLAR. Why?

NATHAN.   That her lips may cling to this dear
speck;
For at her benefactor's feet to fall,
I find, she hopes in vain.

TEMPLAR.   But, jew, your name
You said was Nathan—Nathan, you can join
Your words together cunningly—right well—
I am confused—in fact—I would have been—

NATHAN. Twist, writhe, disguise you, as you will, I know you,
You were too honest, knight, to be more civil;
A girl all feeling, and a she-attendant
All complaisance, a father at a distance—
You valued her good name, and would not see her.
You scorn'd to try her, lest you should be victor;
For that I also thank you.

TEMPLAR.   I confess,
You know how templars ought to think.

NATHAN.   Still templars—
And only *ought* to think—and all because
The rules and vows enjoin it to the *order*—
I know how good men think—know that all lands
Produce good men.

TEMPLAR.   But not without distinction.

NATHAN. In color, dress, and shape, perhaps, distinguish'd.

TEMPLAR. Here more, there fewer sure?

NATHAN.   That boots not much.
The great man everywhere has need of room.
Too many set together only serve
To crush each others' branches. Middling good,

As we are, spring up everywhere in plenty.
Only let one not scar and bruise the other;
Let not the gnarl be angry with the stump;
Let not the upper branch alone pretend
Not to have started from the common earth.
   TEMPLAR. Well said: and yet, I trust, you know the nation,
That first began to strike at fellow men,
That first baptiz'd itself the chosen people—
How now if I were—not to hate this people,
Yet for its pride could not forbear to scorn it,
The pride which it to mussulman and christian
Bequeath'd, as were its God alone the true one.
You start, that I, a christian, and a templar,
Talk thus. Where, when, has e'er the pious rage
To own the better god—on the whole world
To force this better, as the best of all—
Shown itself more, and in a blacker form,
Than here, than now? To him, whom, here and now,
The film is not removing from his eye—
But be he blind that wills! Forget my speeches
And leave me.
   NATHAN.   Ah! indeed you do not know
How closer I shall cling to you henceforth.
We must, we will be friends. Despise my nation—
We did not choose a nation for ourselves.
Are we our nations? What's a nation then?
Were jews and christians such, e'er they were men?
And have I found in thee one more, to whom
It is enough to be a man.
   TEMPLAR.   That hast thou.
Nathan, by God, thou hast. Thy hand. I blush
To have mistaken thee a single instant.
   NATHAN. And I am proud of 't. Only common souls
We seldom err in.
   TEMPLAR.   And uncommon ones
Seldom forget. Yes, Nathan, yes we must,
We will be friends.
   NATHAN.   We are so. And my Recha—
She will rejoice. How sweet the wider prospect,
That dawns upon me! Do but know her—once.
   TEMPLAR. I am impatient for it. Who is that

Bursts from your house, methinks it is your Daya.

NATHAN. Aye—but so anxiously—

TEMPLAR.   Sure, to our Recha
Nothing has happen'd.

NATHAN, TEMPLAR, *and* DAYA.

DAYA. Nathan, Nathan.

NATHAN.   Well.

DAYA. Forgive me, knight, that I must interrupt you.

NATHAN. What is the matter?

TEMPLAR. What?

DAYA.   The sultan sends—
The sultan wants to see you—in a hurry.
Jesus! the sultan—

NATHAN.   Saladin wants me?
He will be curious to see what wares,
Precious, or new, I brought with me from Persia.
Say there is nothing hardly yet unpack'd.

DAYA. No, no: 'tis not to look at any thing.
He wants to speak to you, to you in person,
And orders you to come as soon as may be.

NATHAN. I'll go—return.

DAYA.   Knight, take it not amiss;
But we were so alarm'd for what the sultan
Could have in view.

NATHAN.   That I shall soon discover.

NATHAN *and* TEMPLAR.

TEMPLAR. And don't you know him yet, I mean his person?

NATHAN. Whose, Saladin's? Not yet. I've neither shunn'd,
Nor sought to see him. And the general voice
Speaks too well of him, for me not to wish,
Rather to take its language upon trust,
Than sift the truth out. Yet—if it be so—
He, by the saving of your life, has now—

TEMPLAR. Yes: it is so. The life I live he gave.

NATHAN. And in it double treble life to me.
This flings a bond about me, which shall tie me
For ever to his service: and I scarcely
Like to defer enquiring for his wishes.
For every thing I'm ready; and am ready

To own that 'tis on your account I am so.

TEMPLAR. As often as I've thrown me in his way,
I have not found as yet the means to thank him.
Th' impression that I made upon him came
Quickly, and so has vanish'd. Now perhaps
He recollects me not, who knows? Once more
At least, he must recall me to his mind,
Fully to fix my doom. 'Tis not enough
That by his order I am yet in being,
By his permission live, I have to learn
According to whose will I must exist.

NATHAN. Therefore I shall the more avoid delay.
Perchance some word may furnish me occasion
To glance at you—perchance—Excuse me, knight,
I am in haste. When shall we see you with us?

TEMPLAR. Soon as I may.

NATHAN. That is, whene'er you will.

TEMPLAR. To-day then.

NATHAN. And your name?

TEMPLAR.   My name was—is
Conrade of Stauffen.

NATHAN.   Conrade of Stauffen! Stauffen!

TEMPLAR. Why does that strike so forcibly upon you?

NATHAN. There are more races of that name, no doubt.

TEMPLAR. Yes many of that name were here—rot here.
My uncle even—I should say, my father.
But wherefore is your look so sharpen'd on me?

NATHAN. Nothing—how can I weary to behold you—

TEMPLAR. Therefore I quit you first. The searching eye
Finds often more than it desires to see.
I fear it, Nathan. Fare thee well. Let time,
Not curiosity make us acquainted.

[*Goes.*

NATHAN, *and soon after,* DAYA.

NATHAN. "The searching eye will oft discover more
Than it desires," 'tis as he read my soul.
That too may chance to me. 'Tis not alone
Leonard's walk, stature, but his very voice.
Leonard so wore his head, was even wont
Just so to brush his eye-brows with his hand,

As if to mask the fire that fills his look.
Those deeply graven images at times
How they will slumber in us, seem forgotten,
When all at once a word, a tone, a gesture,
Retraces all. Of Stauffen? Aye right—right—
Filnek and Stauffen—I will soon know more—
But first to Saladin—Ha, Daya there?
Why on the watch? Come nearer. By this time,
I'll answer for't, you've something more at heart
Than to know what the sultan wants with me.

DAYA. And do you take it in ill part of her?
You were beginning to converse with him
More confidentially, just as the message,
Sent by the sultan, tore us from the window.

NATHAN. Go tell her that she may expect his visit
At every instant.

DAYA. What indeed—indeed?

NATHAN. I think I can rely upon thee, Daya:
Be on thy guard, I beg. Thou'lt not repent it.
Be but discreet. Thy conscience too will surely
Find its account in't. Do not mar my plans
But leave them to themselves. Relate and question
With modesty, with backwardness.

DAYA.   O fear not.
How come you to preach up all this to me?
I go—go too. The sultan sends for you
A second time, and by your friend Al-Hafi.

NATHAN *and* HAFI.

HAFI. Ha! art thou here? I was now seeking for thee.

NATHAN. Why in such haste? What wants he then with me?

HAFI. Who?

NATHAN. Saladin. I'm coming—I am coming.

HAFI. Where, to the sultan's?

NATHAN.   Was't not he who sent thee?

HAFI. Me? No. And has he sent already?

NATHAN.   Yes.

HAFI. Then 'tis all right.

NATHAN. What's right?

HAFI.   That I'm unguilty.
God knows I am not guilty, knows I said—

What said I not of thee—belied thee—slander'd—
To ward it off.

    NATHAN. To ward off what—be plain.

    HAFI. That thou art now become his defterdar.
I pity thee. Behold it I will not.
I go this very hour—my road I told thee.
Now—hast thou orders by the way—command,
And then, adieu. Indeed they must not be
Such business as a naked man can't carry.
Quick, what's thy pleasure?

    NATHAN.   Recollect yourself.
As yet all this is quite a riddle to me.
I know of nothing.

    HAFI.   Where are then thy bags?

    NATHAN. Bags?

    HAFI.   Bags of money: bring the weightiest
forth:
The money thou'rt to lend the sultan, Nathan.

    NATHAN. And is that all?

    HAFI.   Novice, thou'st yet to learn
How he day after day will scoop and scoop,
Till nothing but an hollow empty paring.
A husk as light as film, is left behind.
Thou'st yet to learn how prodigality
From prudent bounty's never-empty coffers
Borrows and borrows, till there's not a purse
Left to keep rats from starving. Thou mayst fancy
That he who wants thy gold will heed thy counsel;
But when has he yet listen'd to advice?
Imagine now what just befell me with him.

    NATHAN. Well—

    HAFI.   I went in and found him with his sister,
Engag'd, or rather rising up from chess.
Sittah plays—not amiss. Upon the board
The game, that Saladin suppos'd was lost
And had given up, yet stood. When I drew nigh,
And had examin'd it, I soon discover'd
It was not gone by any means.

    NATHAN.   For you
A blest discovery, a treasure-trove.

    HAFI. He only needed to remove his king

Behind the tower t' have got him out of check.
Could I but make you sensible—
    NATHAN.   I'll trust thee.
    HAFI. Then with the knight still left.—I would have shown
him
And call'd him to the board—He must have won;
But what d'ye think he did?
    NATHAN.   Dar'd doubt your insight?
    HAFI. He would not listen; but with scorn o'erthrew
The standing pieces.
    NATHAN.   Is that possible?
    HAFI. And said, he chose to be check-mate—he chose it
Is that to play the game?
    NATHAN.   Most surely not:
'Tis to play with the game.
    HAFI.   And yet the stake
Was not a nut-shell.
    NATHAN.   Money here or there
Matters but little. Not to listen to thee,
And on a point of such importance, Hafi,
There lies the rub. Not even to admire
Thine eagle eye—thy comprehensive glance—
That calls for vengeance:—does it not, Al-Hafi?
    HAFI. I only tell it thee that thou mayst see
How his brain's form'd. I bear with him no longer.
Here I've been running to each dirty moor,
Inquiring who will lend him. I, who ne'er
Went for myself a begging, go a borrowing,
And that for others. Borrowing's much the same
As begging; just as lending upon usury
Is much the same as thieving—decency
Makes not of lewdness virtue. On the Ganges,
Among my ghebers, I have need of neither:
Nor need I be the tool or pimp of either—
Upon the Ganges only there are men.
Here, thou alone art somehow almost worthy
To have liv'd upon the Ganges. Wilt thou with me?
And leave him with the captive cloak alone,
The booty that he wants to strip thee of.
Little by little he will flay thee clean.
Thus thou 'lt be quit at once, without the tease

Of being slic'd to death. Come wilt thou with me?
I'll find thee with a staff.

    NATHAN.   I should have thought,
Come what come may, that thy resource remain'd:
But I'll consider of it. Stay.

    HAFI.   Consider—
No; such things must not be consider'd.

    NATHAN.   Stay:
Till I have seen the sultan—till you've had—

    HAFI. He, who considers, looks about for motives
To forbear daring. He, who can't resolve
In storm and sunshine to himself to live,
Must live the slave of others all his life.
But, as you please; farewell! 'tis you, who choose.
My path lies yonder—and yours there—

    NATHAN.   Al-Hafi,
Stay then; at least you'll set things right—not leave them
At sixes and at sevens—

    HAFI.   Farce! Parade!
The balance in the chest will need no telling.
And my account—Sittah, or you, will vouch.
Farewell.   [*Goes.*

    NATHAN.   Yes I will vouch it. Honest, wild—
How shall I call you—Ah! the real beggar
Is, after all, the only real monarch.

ACT III.

SCENE.—*A Room in Nathan's House.*

RECHA *and* DAYA.

RECHA. What, Daya, did my father really say
I might expect him, every instant, here?
That meant—now did it not? he would come soon.
And yet how many instants have rolled by!—
But who would think of those that are elapsed?—
To the next moment only I'm alive.—
At last the very one will come that brings him.

DAYA. But for the sultan's ill-tim'd message, Nathan
Had brought him in.

RECHA.   And when this moment comes,
And when this warmest inmost of my wishes
Shall be fulfill'd, what then? what then?

DAYA.   What then?
Why then I hope the warmest of my wishes
Will have its turn, and happen.

RECHA.   'Stead of this,
What wish shall take possession of my bosom,
Which now without some ruling wish of wishes
Knows not to heave? Shall nothing? ah I shudder.

DAYA. Yes: mine shall then supplant the one fulfill'd—
My wish to see thee plac'd one day in Europe
In hands well worthy of thee.

RECHA.   No, thou errest—
The very thing that makes thee form this wish
Prevents its being mine. The country draws thee,
And shall not mine retain me? Shall an image,
A fond remembrance of thy home, thy kindred,
Which years and distance have not yet effac'd,

44

Be mightier o'er thy soul, than what I hear,
See, feel, and hold, of mine?
  DAYA.   'Tis vain to struggle
The ways of heaven are the ways of heaven.
Is he the destin'd saviour, by whose arm
His God, for whom he fights, intends to lead thee
Into the land, which thou wast born for—
  RECHA.   Daya,
What art thou prating of? My dearest Daya,
Indeed thou hast some strange unseemly notions.
"*His* God—*for* whom he fights"—what is a God
Belonging to a man—needing another
To fight his battles? And can we pronounce
For which among the scatter'd clods of earth
You, I was born; unless it be for that
On which we were produced. If Nathan heard thee—
What has my father done to thee, that thou
Hast ever sought to paint my happiness
As lying far remote from him, and his.
What has he done to thee that thus, among
The seeds of reason, which he sow'd unmix'd,
Pure in my soul, thou ever must be seeking
To plant the weeds, or flowers, of thy own land.
He wills not of these pranking gaudy blossoms
Upon this soil. And I too must acknowledge
I feel as if they had a sour-sweet odor,
That makes me giddy—that half suffocates.
Thy head is wont to bear it. I don't blame
Those stronger nerves, that can support it. Mine—
Mine it behooves not. Latterly thy angel
Had made me half a fool. I am asham'd,
Whene'er I see my father, of the folly.
  DAYA. As if here only wisdom were at home—
Folly—if I dar'd speak.
  RECHA.   And dar'st thou not?
When was I not all ear, if thou beganst
To talk about the heroes of thy faith?
Have I not freely on their deeds bestow'd
My admiration, to their sufferings yielded
The tribute of my tears? Their faith indeed
Has never seem'd their most heroic side

To me: yet, therefore, have I only learnt
To find more consolation in the thought,
That our devotion to the God of all
Depends not on our notions about God.
My father has so often told us so—
Thou hast so often to this point consented—
How can it be that thou alone art restless
To undermine what you built up together?
This is not the most fit discussion, Daya,
To usher in our friend to; tho' indeed
I should not disincline to it—for to me
It is of infinite importance if
He too—but hark—there's some one at the door.
If it were he—stay—hush—

                         (A Slave who shows in the Templar).

   They are—here this way.

      Templar, Daya, *and* Recha.

   Recha   *(starts—composes herself—then offers to fall
at his feet.)*
'Tis he—my saviour! ah!
   Templar.   This to avoid
Have I alone deferr'd my call so long.
   Recha. Yes, at the feet of this proud man, I will
Thank—God alone. The man will have no thanks;
No more than will the bucket, which was busy
In showering watery damps upon the flame!
That was fill'd, emptied—but to me to thee
What boots it? So the man—he too, he too
Was thrust, he knew not how, amid the fire.
I dropt, by chance, into his open arm.
By chance, remain'd there—like a fluttering spark
Upon his mantle—till—I know not what
Push'd us both from amid the conflagration.
What room is here for thanks? How oft in Europe
Wine urges men to very different deeds!
Templars must so behave: it is their office,
Like better taught or rather handier spaniels,
To fetch from out of fire, as out of water.
   Templar. O Daya, Daya, if, in hasty moments
Of care and of chagrin, my uncheck'd temper

Betray'd me into rudeness, why convey
To her each idle word that left my tongue?
This is too piercing a revenge indeed;
Yet if henceforth thou wilt interpret better——

DAYA. I question if these barbed words, Sir Knight,
Alighted so, as to have much disserv'd you.

RECHA. How, you had cares, and were more covetous
Of them than of your life?

TEMPLAR   *(who has been viewing her with wonder and
perturbation).*

                              Thou best of beings,
How is my soul 'twixt eye and ear divided!
No: 'twas not she I snatch'd from amid fire:
For who could know her and forbear to do it?——
Indeed——disguis'd by terror——

                              *[Pause: during which he gazes on
her as it were intranc'd.*

RECHA.   But to me
You still appear the same you then appear'd.

                              *[Another like pause—till she resumes,
in order to interrupt him.*

Now tell me, knight, where have you been so long?
It seems as might I ask—where are you now?

TEMPLAR. I am—where I perhaps ought not to be.

RECHA. Where have you been? where you perhaps ought not—
That is not well.

TEMPLAR.   Up—how d'ye call the mountain?
Up Sinai.

RECHA.   Oh that's very fortunate.
Now I shall learn for certain, if 'tis true——

TEMPLAR. What! If the spot may yet be seen where Moses
Stood before God; when first——

RECHA.   No, no, not that.
Where'er he stood, 'twas before God. Of this
I know enough already. Is it true,
I wish to learn from you, that—that it is not
By far so troublesome to climb this mountain
As to get down—for on all mountains else,
That I have seen, quite the reverse obtains.
Well, knight, why will you turn away from me?
Not look at me?

TEMPLAR.   Because I wish to hear you.
RECHA. Because you do not wish me to perceive
You smile at my simplicity—You smile
That I can think of nothing more important
To ask about the holy hill of hills:
Do you not?
TEMPLAR.   Must I meet those eyes again?
And now you cast them down, and damp the smile—
Am I in doubtful motions of the features
To read what I so plainly hear—what you
So audibly declare; yet will conceal?—
How truly said thy father "Do but know her!"
RECHA. Who has—of whom—said so to thee?
TEMPLAR.   Thy father
Said to me "Do but know her" and of thee.
DAYA. And have not I too said so, times and oft.
TEMPLAR. But where is then your father—with the sultan?
RECHA. So I suppose.
TEMPLAR.   Yet there? Oh, I forget,
He cannot be there still. He is waiting for me
Most certainly below there by the cloister.
'Twas so, I think, we had agreed. Forgive,
I go in quest of him.
DAYA.   Knight I'll do that
Wait here, I'll bring him hither instantly.
TEMPLAR. Oh no—Oh no. He is expecting me.
Besides—you are not aware what may have happen'd.
'Tis not unlikely he may be involv'd
With Saladin—you do not know the sultan—
In some unpleasant—I must go, there's danger
If I forbear.
RECHA.   Danger—of what? of what?
TEMPLAR. Danger for me, for thee, for him; unless
I go at once.   [*Goes.*

RECHA *and* DAYA.

RECHA.   What is the matter, Daya?
So quick—what comes across him, drives him hence?
DAYA. Let him alone, I think it no bad sign,
RECHA. Sign—and of what?
DAYA.   That something passes in him.

It boils—but it must not boil over. Leave him—
Now 'tis your turn.
    RECHA.   My turn? Thou dost become
Like him incomprehensible to me.
    DAYA. Now you may give him back all that unrest
He once occasion'd. Be not too severe,
Nor too vindictive.
    RECHA.   Daya, what you mean
You must know best.
    DAYA.   And pray are you again
So calm.
    RECHA.   I am—yes that I am.
    DAYA.   A least
Own—that this restlessness has given you pleasure,
And that you have to thank his want of ease
For what of ease you now enjoy.
    RECHA.   Of that
I am unconscious. All I could confess
Were, that it does seem strange unto myself,
How, in this bosom, such a pleasing calm
Can suddenly succeed to such a tossing.
    DAYA. His countenance, his speech, his manner has
By this time satiated thee.
    RECHA.   Satiated,
I will not say—not by a good deal yet.
    DAYA. But satisfied the more impatient craving.
    RECHA. Well well if you must have it so.
    DAYA.   I? no.
    RECHA. To me he will be ever dear, will ever
Remain more dear than my own life; altho'
My pulse no longer flutters at his name,
My heart no longer, when I think about him,
Beats stronger, swifter. What have I been prating?
Come, Daya, let us once more to the window
Which overlooks the palms.
    DAYA.   So that 'tis not
Yet satisfied—the more impatient craving.
    RECHA. Now I shall see the palm-trees once again,
Not him alone amid them.
    DAYA.   This cold fit
Is but the harbinger of other fevers.

RECHA. Cold—cold—I am not cold; but I observe not
Less willingly what I behold with calmness.

SCENE.—*An Audience Room in the Sultan's Palace.*

SITTAH: SALADIN *giving directions at the door.*

SALADIN. Here, introduce the jew, whene'er he comes—
He seems in no great haste.
SITTAH.   May be at first
He was not in the way.
SALADIN.   Ah, sister, sister!
SITTAH. You seem as if a combat were impending.
SALADIN. With weapons that I have not learnt to wield.
Must I disguise myself? I use precautions?
I lay a snare? When, where gain'd I that knowledge?
And this, for what? To fish for money—money—
For money from a jew—and to such arts
Must Saladin descend at last to come at
The least of little things?
SITTAH.   Each little thing
Despis'd too much finds methods of revenge.
SALADIN. 'Tis but too true. And if this jew should prove
The fair good man, as once the dervis painted—
SITTAH. Then difficulties cease. A snare concerns
The avaricious, cautious, fearful jew;
And not the good wise man: for he is ours
Without a snare. Then the delight of hearing
How such a man speaks out; with what stern strength.
He tears the net, or with what prudent foresight
He one by one undoes the tangled meshes;
That will be all to boot—
SALADIN.   That I shall joy in.
SITTAH. What then should trouble thee? For if he be
One of the many only, a mere jew,
You will not blush to such a one to seem
A man, as he thinks all mankind to be.
One, that to him should bear a better aspect,
Would seem a fool—a dupe.
SALADIN.   So that I must

Act badly, lest the bad think badly of me.
　　SITTAH. Yes, if you call it acting badly, brother,
To use a thing after its kind.
　　SALADIN. 　　　　　There's nothing,
That woman's wit invents, it can't embellish.
　　SITTAH. Embellish—
　　SALADIN. 　　　　　But their fine-wrought filligree
In my rude hand would break. It is for those
That can contrive them to employ such weapons:
They ask a practis'd wrist. But chance what may,
Well as I can—
　　SITTAH. 　　　　　Trust not yourself too little.
I answer for you, if you have the will.
Such men as you would willingly persuade us
It was their swords, their swords alone that rais'd them.
The lion's apt to be asham'd of hunting
In fellowship of the fox—'tis of his fellow
Not of the cunning that he is asham'd.
　　SALADIN. You women would so gladly level man
Down to yourselves. Go, I have got my lesson.
　　SITTAH. What—*must* I go?
　　SALADIN. 　　　　　Had you the thought of staying?
　　SITTAH. In your immediate presence not indeed;
But in the by-room.
　　SALADIN. 　　　　　You could like to listen.
Not that, my sister, if I may insist.
Away! the curtain rustles—he is come.
Beware of staying—I'll be on the watch.

　　*While Sittah retires thro' one door, Nathan enters at another, and
　　　　　　　Saladin seats himself.*

　　　　　　SALADIN *and* NATHAN.

　　SALADIN. Draw nearer, jew, yet nearer; here, quite by me,
Without all fear.
　　NATHAN. 　　　　　Remain that for thy foes!
　　SALADIN. Your name is Nathan?
　　NATHAN. Yes.
　　SALADIN. 　　　　　Nathan the wise?
　　NATHAN. No.
　　SALADIN. 　　　　　If not thou, the people calls thee so.

NATHAN. May be, the people.

SALADIN.   Fancy not that I
Think of the people's voice contemptuously;
I have been wishing much to know the man,
Whom it has nam'd the wise.

NATHAN.   And if it nam'd
Him so in scorn. If wise meant only prudent.
And prudent, one, who knows his interest well.

SALADIN. Who knows his real interest, thou must mean.

NATHAN. Then were the interested, the most prudent,
Then wise and prudent were the same.

SALADIN.   I hear
You proving, what your speeches contradict
You know man's real interests, which the people
Knows not—at least have studied how to know them.
That alone makes the sage.

NATHAN.   Which each imagines
Himself to be.

SALADIN. Of modesty enough!
Ever to meet it, where one seeks to hear
Dry truth, is vexing. Let us to the purpose—
But, jew, sincere and open—

NATHAN.   I will serve thee
So as to merit, prince, thy further notice.

SALADIN. Serve me—how?

NATHAN.   Thou shalt have the best I bring,
Shalt have them cheap.

SALADIN. What speak you of—your wares?
My sister shall be called to bargain with you
For them (so much for the sly listener) I
Have nothing to transact now with the merchant.

NATHAN. Doubtless then you would learn, what, on my journey,
I notic'd of the motions of the foe,
Who stirs anew. If unreserv'd I may—

SALADIN. Neither was that the object of my sending:
I know what I have need to know already.
In short I will'd your presence—

NATHAN.   Sultan, order.

SALADIN. To gain instruction quite on other points.
Since you are a man so wise, tell me which law,

Which faith appears to you the better?

NATHAN.   Sultan,
I am a jew.

SALADIN.   And I a mussulman:
The christian stands between us. Of these three
Religions only one can be the true.
A man, like you, remains not, just where birth
Has chanc'd to cast him, or, if he remains there,
Does it from insight, choice, from grounds of preference.
Share then with me your insight—let me hear
The grounds of preference, which I have wanted
The leisure to examine—learn the choice,
These grounds have motiv'd, that it may be mine.
In confidence I ask it. How you startle,
And weigh me with your eye! It may well be
I'm the first sultan, to whom this caprice,
Methinks not quite unworthy of a sultan,
Has yet occurr'd. Am I not? Speak then—Speak.
Or do you, to collect yourself, desire
Some moments of delay—I give them you—
(Whether she's listening?—I must know of her
If I've done right.) Reflect—I'll soon return—

                              [*Saladin steps into the room to which
Sittah had retired.

NATHAN. Strange! how is this? what wills the sultan of me?
I came prepar'd with cash—he asks truth. Truth?
As if truth too were cash—a coin disus'd
That goes by weight—indeed 'tis some such thing—
But a new coin, known by the stamp at once,
To be flung down and told upon the counter,
It is not that. Like gold in bags tied up,
So truth lies hoarded in the wise man's head
To be brought out—Which now in this transaction
Which of us plays the jew; he asks for truth,
Is truth what he requires, his aim, his end?
That this is but the glue to lime a snare
Ought not to be suspected, 'twere too little,
Yet what is found too little for the great—
In fact, thro' hedge and pale to stalk at once
Into one's field beseems not—friends look round,
Seek for the path, ask leave to pass the gate—

I must be cautious. Yet to damp him back,
And be the stubborn jew is not the thing;
And wholly to throw off the jew, still less.
For if no jew he might with right inquire—
Why not a mussulman—Yes—that may serve me.
Not children only can be quieted
With stories. Ha! he comes—well, let him come.

SALADIN *(returning)*. So, there, the field is clear, I'm not too quick,
Thou hast bethought thyself as much as need is,
Speak, no one hears.

NATHAN.   Might the whole world but hear us.

SALADIN. Is Nathan of his cause so confident?
Yes, that I call the sage—to veil no truth,
For truth to hazard all things, life and goods.

NATHAN. Aye, when 'tis necessary and when useful.

SALADIN. Henceforth I hope I shall with reason bear
One of my titles—"Betterer of the world
And of the law."

NATHAN.   In truth a noble title.
But, sultan, e'er I quite unfold myself
Allow me to relate a tale.

SALADIN.   Why not?
I always was a friend of tales well told.

NATHAN. Well told, that's not precisely my affair.

SALADIN. Again so proudly modest, come begin.

NATHAN. In days of yore, there dwelt in east a man,
Who from a valued hand receiv'd a ring
Of endless worth: the stone of it an opal,
That shot an ever-changing tint: moreover,
It had the hidden virtue him render.
Of God and man belov'd, who in this view
And this persuasion, wore it. Was it strange
The eastern man ne'er drew it off his finger,
And studiously provided to secure it
For ever to his house. Thus—He bequeath'd it;
First, to the *most beloved* of his sons,
Ordain'd that he again should leave the ring
To the *most dear* among his children—and
That without heeding birth, the *favourite* son,
In virtue of the ring alone, should always

Remain the lord o' th' house—You hear me, sultan?

    SALADIN. I understand thee—on.

    NATHAN.   From son to son,

At length this ring descended to a father,

Who had three sons, alike obedient to him;

Whom therefore he could not but love alike.

At times seem'd this, now that, at times the third,

(Accordingly as each apart receiv'd

The overflowings of his heart) most worthy

To heir the ring, which with goodnatur'd weakness

He privately to each in turn had promis'd.

This went on for a while. But death approach'd,

And the good father grew embarrass'd. So

To dissapoint two sons, who trust his promise,

He could not bear. What's to be done. He sends

In secret to a jeweller, of whom,

Upon the model of the real ring,

He might bespeak two others, and commanded

To spare nor cost nor pains to make them like,

Quite like the true one. This the artist manag'd.

The rings were brought, and e'en the father's eye

Could not distinguish which had been the model.

Quite overjoy'd he summons all his sons,

Takes leave of each apart, on each bestows

His blessing and his ring, and dies—Thou hearst me?

    SALADIN. I hear, I hear, come finish with thy tale;

Is it soon ended?

    NATHAN.   It is ended, sultan,

For all that follows may be guess'd of course.

Scarce is the father dead, each with his ring

Appears, and claims to be the lord o' th' house.

Comes question, strife, complaint—all to no end;

For the true ring could no more be distinguish'd

Than now can—the true faith.

    SALADIN.   How, how, is that

To be the answer to my query?

    NATHAN.   No,

But it may serve as my apology;

If I can't venture to decide between

Rings, which the father got expressly made,

That they might not be known from one another.

SALADIN. The rings—don't trifle with me; I must think
That the religions which I nam'd can be
Distinguish'd, e'en to raiment, drink and food.

NATHAN. And only not as to their grounds of proof.
Are not all built alike on history,
Traditional, or written. History
Must be received on trust—is it not so?
In whom now are we likeliest to put trust?
In our own people surely, in those men
Whose blood we are, in them who from our childhood
Have given us proofs of love, who ne'er deceiv'd us,
Unless 'twere wholesomer to be deceiv'd.
How can I less believe in my forefathers
Than thou in thine. How can I ask of thee
To own that thy forefathers falsified
In order to yield mine the praise of truth.
The like of christians.

SALADIN.   By the living God,
The man is in the right, I must be silent.

NATHAN. Now let us to our rings return once more.
As said, the sons complain'd. Each to the judge
Swore from his father's hand immediately
To have receiv'd the ring, as was the case;
After he had long obtain'd the father's promise,
One day to have the ring, as also was.
The father, each asserted, could to him
Not have been false, rather than so suspect
Of such a father, willing as he might be
With charity to judge his brethren, he
Of treacherous forgery was bold t' accuse them.

SALADIN. Well, and the judge, I'm eager now to hear
What thou wilt make him say. Go on, go on.

NATHAN. The judge said, if ye summon not the father
Before my seat, I cannot give a sentence.
Am I to guess enigmas? Or expect ye
That the true ring should here unseal its lips?
But hold—you tell me that the real ring
Enjoys the hidden power to make the wearer
Of God and man belov'd; let that decide.
Which of you do two brothers love the best?
You're silent. Do these love-exciting rings

Act inward only, not without? Does each
Love but himself? Ye're all deceiv'd deceivers,
None of your rings is true. The real ring
Perhaps is gone. To hide or to supply
Its loss, your father order'd three for one.

  SALADIN. O charming, charming!
  NATHAN.   And (the judge continued)
If you will take advice in lieu of sentence,
This is my counsel to you, to take up
The matter where it stands. If each of you
Has had a ring presented by his father,
Let each believe his own the real ring.
'Tis possible the father chose no longer
To tolerate the one ring's tyranny;
And certainly, as he much lov'd you all,
And lov'd you all alike, it could not please him
By favouring one to be of two th' oppressor.
Let each feel honour'd by this affection
Unwarp'd of prejudice; let each endeavour
To vie with both his brothers in displaying
The virtue of his ring; assist its might
With gentleness, benevolence, forbearance,
With inward resignation to the godhead,
And if the virtues of the ring continue
To show themselves among your children's children,
After a thousand thousand years, appear
Before this judgment-seat—a greater one
Than I shall sit upon it, and decide.
So spake the modest judge.

  SALADIN.   God!
  NATHAN.   Saladin,
Feelst thou thyself this wiser, promis'd man?
  SALADIN. I dust, I nothing, God!
[Precipitates himself upon Nathan and takes hold of his hand, which he
does not quit the remainder of the scene.
  NATHAN.   What moves thee, sultan?
  SALADIN. Nathan, my dearest Nathan, 'tis not yet
The judge's thousand thousand years are past,
His judgment-seat's not mine. Go, go, but love me.
  NATHAN. Has Saladin then nothing else to order?
  SALADIN. No.

NATHAN. Nothing?

SALADIN.   Nothing in the least, and wherefore?

NATHAN. I could have wish'd an opportunity
To lay a prayer before you.

SALADIN.   Is there need
Of opportunity for that? Speak freely.

NATHAN. I come from a long journey from collecting
Debts, and I've almost of hard cash too much;
The times look perilous—I know not where
To lodge it safely—I was thinking thou,
For coming wars require large sums, couldst use it.

SALADIN *(fixing Nathan)*. Nathan, I ask not if thou sawst Al-Hafi,
I'll not examine if some shrewd suspicion
Spurs thee to make this offer of thyself.

NATHAN. Suspicion—

SALADIN.   I deserve this offer. Pardon,
For what avails concealment, I acknowledge
I was about—

NATHAN. To ask the same of me?

SALADIN. Yes.

NATHAN.   Then 'tis well we're both accommodated.
That I can't send thee all I have of treasure
Arises from the templar; thou must know him,
I have a weighty debt to pay to him.

SALADIN. A templar! How, thou dost not with thy gold
Support my direst foes.

NATHAN.   I speak of him
Whose life the sultan—

SALADIN.   What art thou recalling?
I had forgot the youth, whence is he, knowest thou?

NATHAN. Hast thou not heard then how thy clemency
To him has fallen on me. He at the risk
Of his new-spar'd existence, from the flames
Rescued my daughter.

SALADIN.   Ha! Has he done that?
He look'd like one that would—my brother too,
Whom he's so like, had done it. Is he here still?
Bring him to me—I have so often talk'd
To Sittah of this brother, whom she knew not,
That I must let her see his counterfeit.
Go fetch him. How a single worthy action,

Though but of whim or passion born, gives rise
To other blessings! Fetch him.
   NATHAN.   In an instant.
The rest remains as settled.
   SALADIN.   O, I wish
I had let my sister listen. Well, I'll to her.
How shall I make her privy to all this?

SCENE.—*The Place of Palms.*

The TEMPLAR *walking and agitated.*

   TEMPLAR. Here let the weary victim pant awhile.—
Yet would I not have time to ascertain
What passes in me; would not snuff beforehand
The coming storm. 'Tis sure I fled in vain;
But more than fly I could not do, whatever
Comes of it. Ah! to ward it off—the blow
Was given so suddenly. Long, much, I strove
To keep aloof; but vainly. Once to see her—
Her, whom I surely did not court the sight of,
To see her, and to form the resolution,
Never to lose sight of her here again,
Was one—The resolution?—Not 'tis will,
Fixt purpose, made (for I was passive in it)
Seal'd, doom'd. To see her, and to feel myself
Bound to her, wove into her very being,
Was one—remains one. Separate from her
To live is quite unthinkable—is death.
And wheresoever after death we be,
There too the thought were death. And is this love?
Yet so in troth the templar loves—so—so—
The christian loves the jewess. What of that?
Here in this holy land, and therefore holy
And dear to me, I have already doff'd
Some prejudices.—Well—what says my vow?
As templar I am dead, was dead to that
From the same hour which made me prisoner
To Saladin. But is the head, he gave me,
My old one? No. It knows no word of what
Was prated into yon, of what had bound it.

It is a better; for its patrial sky
Fitter than yon. I feel—I'm conscious of it.
With this I now begin to think, as here
My father must have thought; if tales of him
Have not been told untruly. Tales—why tales?
They're credible—more credible than ever—
Now that I'm on the brink of stumbling, where
He fell. He fell? I'd rather fall with men,
Than stand with children. His example pledges
His approbation, and whose approbation
Have I else need of? Nathan's? Surely of his
Encouragement, applause, I've little need
To doubt—O what a jew is he! yet easy
To pass for the mere jew. He's coming—swiftly—
And looks delighted—who leaves Saladin
With other looks? Hoa, Nathan!

NATHAN *and* TEMPLAR.

NATHAN.   Are you there?
    TEMPLAR. Your visit to the sultan has been long.
    NATHAN. Not very long; my going was indeed
Too much delay'd. Troth, Conrade, this man's fame
Outstrips him not. His fame is but his shadow.
But before all I have to tell you—
    TEMPLAR.   What?
    NATHAN. That he would speak with you, and that directly.
First to my house, where I would give some orders,
Then we'll together to the sultan.
    TEMPLAR.   Nathan,
I enter not thy doors again before—
    NATHAN. Then you've been there this while—have spoken
with her.
How do you like my Recha?
    TEMPLAR.   Words cannot tell—
Gaze on her once again—I never will—
Never—no never: unless thou wilt promise
That I for ever, ever, may behold her.
    NATHAN. How should I take this?
    TEMPLAR *(falling suddenly upon his neck)*. Nathan—O my father!
    NATHAN. Young man!

TEMPLAR *(quitting him as suddenly).*   Not son?—I pray
thee, Nathan— ha!

NATHAN. Thou dear young man!

TEMPLAR.   Not son?—I pray thee, Nathan,
Conjure thee by the strongest bonds of nature,
Prefer not those of later date, the weaker.—
Be it enough to thee to be a man!
Push me not from thee!

NATHAN.   Dearest, dearest friend!—

TEMPLAR. Not son? Not son? Not even—even if
Thy daughter's gratitude had in her bosom
Prepar'd the way for love—not even if
Both wait thy nod alone to be but one?—
You do not speak?

NATHAN.   Young knight, you have surpriz'd me.

TEMPLAR. Do I surprize thee—thus surprize thee, Nathan,
With thy own thought? Canst thou not in my mouth
Know it again? Do I surprize you?

NATHAN.   Ere
I know, which of the Stauffens was your father?

TEMPLAR. What say you Nathan?—And in such a moment
Is curiosity your only feeling?

NATHAN. For see, once I myself well knew a Stauffen,
Whose name was Conrade.

TEMPLAR.   Well, and if my father
Was bearer of that name?

NATHAN.   Indeed?

TEMPLAR.   My name
Is from my father's, Conrade.

NATHAN.   Then thy father
Was not my Conrade. He was, like thyself,
A templar, never wedded.

TEMPLAR.   For all that—

NATHAN. How?

TEMPLAR.   For all that he may have been
my father.

NATHAN. You joke.

TEMPLAR.   And you are captious. Boots it then
To be true-born? Does bastard wound thine ear?
The race is not to be despis'd: but hold,
Spare me my pedigree; I'll spare thee thine.

Not that I doubt thy genealogic tree.
O, God forbid! You may attest it all
As far as Abraham back; and backwarder
I know it to my heart—I'll swear to it also.
    NATHAN. Knight, you grow bitter. Do I merit this?
Have I refus'd you ought? I've but forborne
To close with you at the first word—no more.
    TEMPLAR. Indeed—no more? O then forgive—
    NATHAN.   'Tis well.
Do but come with me.
    TEMPLAR.   Whither? To thy house?
No; there not—there not: 'tis a burning soil.
Here I await thee, go. Am I again
To see her, I shall see her times enough:
If not I have already gaz'd too much.
    NATHAN. I'll try to be soon back.   [*Goes.*
    TEMPLAR.   Too much indeed—
Strange that the human brain, so infinite
Of comprehension, yet at times will fill
Quite full, and all at once, of a mere trifle—
No matter what it teems with. Patience! Patience!
The soul soon calms again, th' upboiling stuff
Makes itself room and brings back light and order.
Is this then the first time I love? Or was
What by that name I knew before, not love—
And this, this love alone that now I feel?

DAYA *and* TEMPLAR.

    DAYA. Sir knight, sir knight.
    TEMPLAR.   Who calls? ha, Daya, you?
    DAYA. I manag'd to slip by him. No, come here
(He'll see us where you stand) behind this tree.
    TEMPLAR. Why so mysterious? What's the matter, Daya?
    DAYA. Yes, 'tis a secret that has brought me to you.
A twofold secret. One I only know,
The other only you. Let's interchange,
Intrust yours first to me, then I'll tell mine.
    TEMPLAR. With pleasure when I'm able to discover
What you call mine. But that yours will explain.
Begin—

DAYA.   That is not fair, yours first, sir knight;
For be assur'd my secret serves you not
Unless I have yours first. If I sift it out
You'll not have trusted me, and then my secret
Is still my own, and yours lost all for nothing.
But, knight, how can you men so fondly fancy
You ever hide such secrets from us women.

   TEMPLAR. Secrets we often are unconscious of.

   DAYA. May be——So then I must at last be friendly,
And break it to you. Tell me now, whence came it
That all at once you started up abruptly
And in the twinkling of an eye were fled?
That you left us without one civil speech!
That you return no more with Nathan to us——
Has Recha then made such a slight impression,
Or made so deep a one? I penetrate you.
Think you that on a lim'd twig the poor bird
Can flutter cheerfully, or hop at ease
With its wing pinion'd? Come, come, in one word
Acknowledge to me plainly that you love her,
Love her to madness, and I'll tell you what.

   TEMPLAR. To madness, oh, you're very penetrating.

   DAYA. Grant me the love, and I'll give up the madness.

   TEMPLAR. Because that must be understood of course——
A templar love a jewess——

   DAYA.   Seems absurd,
But often there's more fitness in a thing
Than we at once discern; nor were this time
The first, when thro' an unexpected path
The Saviour drew his children on to him
Across the tangled maze of human life.

   TEMPLAR. So solemn that——(and yet if in the stead
Of Saviour, I were to say Providence,
It would sound true) you make me curious, Daya,
Which I'm unwont to be.

   DAYA.   This is the place
For miracles

   TEMPLAR.   For wonders——well and good——
Can it be otherwise, where the whole world
Presses as toward a centre. My dear Daya,

Consider what you ask of me as own'd;
That I do love her—that I can't imagine
How I should live without her—that—

DAYA.   Indeed!
Then, knight, swear to me you will call her yours,
Make both her present and eternal welfare.

TEMPLAR. And how, how can I, can I swear to do
What is not in my power?

DAYA.   'Tis in your power,
A single word will put it in your power.

TEMPLAR. So that her father shall not be against it
DAYA. Her father—father? he shall be compell'd.
TEMPLAR. As yet he is not fallen among thieves—
Compell'd?

DAYA.   Aye to be willing that you should.

TEMPLAR. Compell'd and willing—what if I inform thee
That I have tried to touch this string already,
It vibrates not responsive.

DAYA.   He refus'd thee?

TEMPLAR. He answer'd in a tone of such discordance
That I was hurt.

DAYA.   What do you say? How, you
Betray'd the shadow of a wish for Recha,
And he did not spring up for joy, drew back,
Drew coldly back, made difficulties?

TEMPLAR.   Almost.

DAYA. Well then I'll not deliberate a moment.

TEMPLAR. And yet you are deliberating still.

DAYA. That man was always else so good, so kind,
I am so deeply in his debt. Why, why
Would he not listen to you? God's my witness
That my heart bleeds to come about him thus.

TEMPLAR. I pray you, Daya, once for all, to end
This dire uncertainty. But if you doubt
Whether what 'tis your purpose to reveal
Be right or wrong, be praiseworthy or shameful,
Speak not—I will forget that you have had
Something to hide.

DAYA.   That spurs me on still more.
Then learn that Recha is no jewess, that
She is a christian.

TEMPLAR.   I congratulate you,
'Twas a hard labor, but 'tis out at last;
The pangs of the delivery won't hurt you.
Go on with undiminish'd zeal, and people
Heaven, when no longer fit to people earth.

DAYA. How, knight, does my intelligence deserve
Such bitter scorn? That Recha is a christian
On you, a christian templar, and her lover,
Confers no joy?

TEMPLAR.   Particularly as
She is a christian of your making, Daya.

DAYA. O, so you understand it—well and good—
I wish to find out him that might convert her.
It is her fate long since to have been that
Which she is spoil'd for being.

TEMPLAR.   Do explain—
Or go.

DAYA.   She is a christian child—of christian
Parents was born and is baptiz'd.

TEMPLAR *(hastily)*.   And Nathan—

DAYA. Is not her father.

TEMPLAR.   Nathan not her father—
And are you sure of what you say?

DAYA.   I am,
It is a truth has cost me tears of blood.
No, he is not her father.

TEMPLAR.   And has only
Brought her up as his daughter, educated
The christian child a jewess.

DAYA.   Certainly.

TEMPLAR. And she is unacquainted with her birth?
Has never learnt from him that she was born
A christian, and no jewess?

DAYA.   Never yet.

TEMPLAR. And he not only let the child grow up
In this mistaken notion, but still leaves
The woman in it.

DAYA.   Aye, alas!

TEMPLAR.   How, Nathan,
The wise good Nathan, thus allow himself
To stifle nature's voice? Thus to misguide

Upon himself th' effusions of a heart
Which to itself abandoned would have form'd
Another bias, Daya—yes, indeed
You have intrusted an important secret
That may have consequences—it confounds me,
I cannot tell what I've to do at present,
Therefore go, give me time, he may come by
And may surprize us.

    DAYA.   I should drop for fright.

    TEMPLAR. I am not able now to talk, farewell;
And if you chance to meet him, only say
That we shall find each other at the sultan's.

    DAYA. Let him not see you've any grudge against him.
That should be kept to give the proper impulse
To things at last, and may remove your scruples
Respecting Recha. But then, if you take her
Back with you into Europe, let not me
Be left behind.

    TEMPLAR.   That we'll soon settle, go.

ACT IV.

SCENE—*The Cloister of a Convent*

The FRIAR *alone.*

FRIAR. Aye—aye—he's very right—the patriarch is—
In fact of all that he has sent me after
Not much turns out his way—Why put on me
Such business and no other? I don't care
To coax and wheedle, and to run my nose
Into all sorts of things, and have a hand
In all that's going forward. I did not
Renounce the world, for my own part, in order
To be entangled with 't for other people.

FRIAR *and* TEMPLAR.

TEMPLAR (*abruptly entering*). Good brother are you there? I've
sought you long.
FRIAR. Me, sir?
TEMPLAR.   What don't you recollect me?
FRIAR.   Oh,
I thought I never in my life was likely
To see you any more. For so I hop'd
In God. I did not vastly relish the proposal
That I was bound to make you. Yes, God knows,
How little I desir'd to find a hearing,
Knows I was inly glad when you refus'd
Without a moment's thought, what of a knight
Would be unworthy. Are your second thoughts—
TEMPLAR. So, you already know my purpose, I
Scarce know myself.
FRIAR.   Have you by this reflected

67

That our good patriarch is not so much out,
That gold and fame in plenty may be got
By his commission, that a foe's a foe
Were he our guardian angel seven times over.
Have you weigh'd this 'gainst flesh and blood, and come
To strike the bargain he propos'd. Ah, God.

    TEMPLAR. My dear good man, set your poor heart at ease.
Not therefore am I come, not therefore wish
To see the patriarch in person. Still
On the first point I think as I then thought,
Nor would I for ought in the world exchange
That good opinion, which I once obtain'd
From such a worthy upright man as thou art,
I come to ask your patriarch's advice—

FRIAR *(looking round with timidity)*. Our patriarch's—you? a knight
ask priest's advice?

    TEMPLAR. Mine is a priestly business.

    FRIAR.   Yet the priests
Ask not the knight's advice be their affair
Ever so knightly.

    TEMPLAR.   Therefore one allows them
To overshoot themselves, a privilege
Which such as I don't vastly envy them.
Indeed if I were acting for myself,
Had not t' account with others, I should care
But little for his counsel. But some things
I'd rather do amiss by other's guidance
Than by my own aright. And then by this time
I see religion too is party, and
He, who believes himself the most impartial,
Does but uphold the standard of his own,
Howe'er unconsciously. And since 'tis so,
So must be well.

    FRIAR.   I rather shall not answer,
For I don't understand exactly.

    TEMPLAR.   Yet
Let me consider what it is precisely
That I have need of, counsel or decision,
Simple or learned counsel.—Thank you, brother,
I thank you for your hint—A patriarch—why?
Be thou my patriarch; for 'tis the plain christian,

Whom in the patriarch I have to consult,
And not the patriarch in the christian.
    FRIAR.   Oh,
I beg no further—you must quite mistake me;
He that knows much hath learnt much care, and I
Devoted me to only one. 'Tis well,
Most luckily here comes, the very man,
Wait here, stand still—he has perceiv'd you, knight.
    TEMPLAR. I'd rather shun him, he is not my man.
A thick red smiling prelate—and as stately—
    FRIAR. But you should see him on a gala-day;
He only comes from visiting the sick.
    TEMPLAR. Great Saladin must then be put to shame.

The Patriarch, after marching up one of the ailes in great pomp, draws
near, and makes signs to the Friar, who approaches him.

PATRIARCH, FRIAR, *and* TEMPLAR.

    PATRIARCH. Hither—was that the templar? What wants he?
    FRIAR. I know not.
    PATRIARCH. *(approaches the templar, while the friar and the rest of*
his train draw back).

                             So, sir knight, I'm truly happy
To meet the brave young man—so very young too—
Something, God helping, may come of him.
    TEMPLAR.   More
Than is already hardly will come of him,
But less, my reverend father, that may chance.
    PATRIARCH. It is my prayer at least a knight so pious
May for the cause of Christendom and God
Long be preserved; nor can that fail, so be
Young valor will lend ear to aged counsel.
With what can I be useful any way?
    TEMPLAR. With that which my youth is without, with counsel.
    PATRIARCH. Most willingly, but counsel should be follow'd.
    TEMPLAR. Surely not blindly?
    PATRIARCH.   Who says that? Indeed
None should omit to make use of the reason
Given him by God, in things where it belongs,
But it belongs not every where; for instance,
If God, by some one of his blessed angels,

Or other holy minister of his word,
Deign'd to make known a mean, by which the welfare
Of Christendom, or of his holy church,
In some peculiar and especial manner
Might be promoted or secured, who then
Shall venture to rise up, and try by reason
The will of him who has created reason,
Measure th' eternal laws of heaven by
The little rules of a vain human honor?—
But of all this enough. What is it then
On which our counsel is desir'd?

TEMPLAR.   Suppose,
My reverend father, that a jew possess'd
An only child, a girl we'll say, whom he
With fond attention forms to every virtue,
And loves more than his very soul; a child
Who by her pious love requites his goodness.
And now suppose it whisper'd—say to me—
This girl is not the daughter of the jew,
He pick'd up, purchas'd, stole her in her childhood—
That she was born of christians and baptiz'd,
But that the jew hath rear'd her as a jewess,
Allows her to remain a jewess, and
To think herself his daughter. Reverend father
What then ought to be done?

PATRIARCH.   I shudder! But
First will you please explain if such a case
Be fact, or only an hypothesis?
That is to say, if you, of your own head,
Invent the case, or if indeed it happen'd,
And still continues happening?

TEMPLAR.   I had thought
That just to learn your reverence's opinion
This were all one.

PATRIARCH.   All one—now see how apt
Proud human reason is in spiritual things
To err: 'tis not all one; for, if the point
In question be a mere sport of the wit,
'Twill not be worth our while to think it thro',
But I should recommend the curious person
To theatres, where oft, with loud applause,

Such pro and contras have been agitated.
But if the object should be something more
Than by a school-trick—by a sleight of logic
To get the better of me—if the case
Be really extant, if it should have happen'd
Within our diocese, or—or perhaps
Here in our dear Jerusalem itself,
Why then—

TEMPLAR.   What then?

PATRIARCH.   Then were it proper
To execute at once upon the jew
The penal laws in such a case provided
By papal and imperial right, against
So foul a crime—such dire abomination.

TEMPLAR. So.

PATRIARCH.   And the laws forementioned have decreed,
That if a jew shall to apostacy
Seduce a christian, he shall die by fire.

TEMPLAR. So.

PATRIARCH.   How much more the jew, who forcibly
Tears from the holy font a christian child,
And breaks the sacramental bond of baptism;
For all what's done to children is by force—
I mean except what the church does to children.

TEMPLAR. What if the child, but for this fostering jew,
Must have expir'd in misery?

PATRIARCH.   That's nothing,
The jew has still deserv'd the faggot—for
'Twere better it here died in misery
Than for eternal woe to live. Besides,
Why should the jew forestall the hand of God?
God, if he wills to save, can save without him.

TEMPLAR. And spite of him too save eternally.

PATRIARCH. That's nothing! Still the jew is to be burnt.

TEMPLAR. That hurts me—more particularly as
'Tis said he has not so much taught the maid
His faith, as brought her up with the mere knowledge
Of what our reason teaches about God.

PATRIARCH. That's nothing! Still the jew is to be burnt—

And for this very reason would deserve
To be thrice burnt. How, let a child grow up
Without a faith? Not even teach a child
The greatest of its duties, to believe?
'Tis heinous! I am quite astonish'd, knight,
That you yourself—

TEMPLAR.   The rest, right reverend sir,
In the confessional, but not before.   [*Offers to go.*

PATRIARCH. What off—not stay for my interrogation—
Not name to me this infidel, this jew—
Not find him up for me at once? But hold,
A thought occurs, I'll straightway to the sultan
Conformably to the capitulation,
Which Saladin has sworn, he must support us
In all the privileges, all the doctrines
Which appertain to our most holy faith,
Thank God, we've the original in keeping,
We have his hand and seal to it—we—
And I shall lead him easily to think
How very dangerous for the state it is
Not to believe. All civic bonds divide,
Like flax fire-touch'd, where subjects don't believe.
Away with foul impiety!

TEMPLAR.   It happens
Somewhat unlucky that I want the leisure
To enjoy this holy sermon. I am sent for
To Saladin.

PATRIARCH. Why then—indeed—if so—

TEMPLAR. And will prepare the sultan, if agreeable,
For your right reverend visit.

PATRIARCH.   I have heard
That you found favor in the sultan's sight,
I beg with all humility to be
Remember'd to him. I am purely motiv'd
By zeal in th' cause of God—What of too much
I do, I do for him—weigh that in goodness.
'Twas then, most noble sir—what you were starting
About the jew—a problem merely!

TEMPLAR.   Problem!
                    [*Goes.*

PATRIARCH. Of whose foundation I'll have nearer knowledge.

Another job for brother Bonafides.
Hither my son!

[*Converses with the Friar as he walks off.*

SCENE.—*A Room in the Palace.*

SLAVES *bring in a number of purses and pile them on the floor.*
SALADIN *is present.*

SALADIN. In troth this has no end. And is there much
Of this same thing behind?
SLAVE.   About one half.
SALADIN. Then take the rest to Sittah. Where's Al-Hafi?
What's here Al-Hafi shall take charge of strait.
Or shan't I rather send it to my father;
Here it slips thro' one's fingers. Sure in time
One may grow callous; it shall now cost labor
To come at much from me—at least until
The treasures come from Ægypt, poverty
Must shift as't can—yet at the sepulcher
The charges must go on—the christian pilgrims
Shall not go back without an alms.

SALADIN *and* SITTAH.

SITTAH *(entering)*.   Why this?
Wherefore the gold to me?
SALADIN.   Pay thyself with it,
And if there's something left 'twill be in store.
Are Nathan and the templar not yet come?
SITTAH. He has been seeking for him everywhere—
Look what I met with when the plate and jewels
Were passing thro' my hands—

                              [*Shewing a small portrait.*
SALADIN.   Ha! What, my brother?
'Tis he, 'tis he, *was* he, *was* he alas!
Thou dear brave youth, and lost to me so early;
What would I not with thee and at thy side
Have undertaken? Let me have the portrait,
I recollect it now again; he gave it
Unto thy elder sister, to his Lilah,

That morning that she would not part with him,
But clasp'd him so in tears. It was the last
Morning that he rode out; and I—I let him
Ride unattended. Lilah died for grief,
And never could forgive me that I let him
Then ride alone. He came not back.
    SITTAH.   Poor brother—
    SALADIN. Time shall be when none of us will come back,
And then who knows? It is not death alone
That balks the hopes of young men of his cast,
Such have far other foes, and oftentimes
The strongest like the weakest is o'ercome.
Be as it may—I must compare this picture
With our young templar, to observe how much
My fancy cheated me.
    SITTAH.   I therefore brought it;
But give it me, I'll tell thee if 'tis like.
We women see that best.
    SALADIN *(to a slave at the door)*.   Ah, who is there?
The templar? let him come.
    SITTAH *(throws herself on a sofa apart and drops her veil)*.
    Not to interfere,
Or with my curiosity disturb you.
    SALADIN. That's right. And then his voice, will that be like?
The tone of Assad's voice, sleeps somewhere yet—
So—

TEMPLAR and SALADIN.

    TEMPLAR. I thy prisoner, sultan.
    SALADIN.   Thou my prisoner—
And shall I not to him whose life I gave
Also give freedom?
    TEMPLAR.   What 'twere worthy thine
To do, it is my part to hear of thee,
And not to take for granted. But, O Sultan,
To lay loud protestations at thy feet
Of gratitude for a life spared, agrees
Not with my station or my character.
At all times, 'tis once more, prince, at thy service.
    SALADIN. Only forbear to use it against me.
Not that I grudge my enemy one pair more

Of hands—but such a heart, it goes against me
To yield him. I have been deceiv'd with thee,
Thou brave young man, in nothing—Yes, thou art
In soul and body Assad. I could ask thee,
Where then hast thou been lurking all this time?
Or in what cavern slept? What Ginnistan
Chose some kind Perie for thy hiding-place,
That she might ever keep the flower thus fresh?
Methinks I could remind thee here and yonder
Of what we did together—could abuse thee
For having had one secret, e'en to me—
Cheat me of one adventure—yes, I could,
If I saw thee alone, and not myself.
Thanks that so much of this fond sweet illusion
At least is true, that in my sear of life
An Assad blossoms for me. Thou art willing?

    Templar. All that from thee comes to me, whatsoever
It chance to prove, lies as a wish already
Within my soul.

    Saladin.   We'll try th' experiment.
Wilt thou stay with me? dwell about me? boots not
As mussulman or christian, in a turban
Or a white mantle—I have never wish'd
To see the same bark grow about all trees.

    Templar. Else, Saladin, thou hardly hadst become
The hero that thou art, alike to all
The gardener of the Lord.

    Saladin.   If thou think not
The worse of me for this, we're half right.

    Templar.   Quite so.

    Saladin (holds out his hand). One word.

    Templar (takes it).   One man—and with this, receive more
Than thou canst take away again—thine wholly.

    Saladin. 'Tis for one day too great a gain—too great.
Came he not with thee?

    Templar. Who?

    Saladin.   Who? Nathan.

    Templar (coldly).   No,
I came alone.

    Saladin.   O what a deed of thine!
And what a happiness, a blessing to thee,

That such a deed was serving such a man.
  TEMPLAR. Yes, yes.
  SALADIN.   So cold—no my young friend—when
God
Does thro' our means a service, we ought not
To be so cold, not out of modesty
Wish to appear so cold.
  TEMPLAR.   In this same world
All things have many sides, and 'tis not easy
To comprehend how they can fit each other.
  SALADIN. Cling ever to the best—Give praise to God,
Who knows how they can fit. But, my young man,
If thou wilt be so difficult, I must
Be very cautious with thee, for I too
Have many sides, and some of them perhaps
Such as mayn't always seem to fit.
  TEMPLAR.   That wounds me;
Suspicion usually is not my failing.
  SALADIN. Say then of whom thou harbour'st it, of Nathan?
So should thy talk imply—canst thou suspect him?
Give me the first proof of thy confidence.
  TEMPLAR. I've nothing against Nathan, I am angry
With myself only.
  SALADIN. And for what?
  TEMPLAR.   For dreaming
That any jew could learn to be no jew—
For dreaming it awake.
  SALADIN.   Out with this dream.
  TEMPLAR. Thou knowst of Nathan's daughter, sultan. What
I did for her I did—because I did it;
Too proud to reap thanks which I had not sown for,
I shunn'd from day to day her very sight.
The father was far off. He comes, he hears,
He seeks me, thanks me, wishes that his daughter
May please me; talks to me of dawning prospects—
I listen to his prate, go, see, and find
A girl indeed. O, sultan, I am asham'd—
  SALADIN. Asham'd that a jew girl knew how to make
Impression on thee, surely not.
  TEMPLAR.   But that
To this impression my rash yielding heart,

Trusting the smoothness of the father's prate,
Oppos'd no more resistance. Fool—I sprang
A second time into the flame, and then
I wooed, and was deny'd.

SALADIN.   Deny'd! Deny'd!

TEMPLAR. The prudent father does not flatly say
No to my wishes, but the prudent father
Must first enquire, and look about, and think.
Oh, by all means. Did not I do the same?
Did not I look about and ask who 'twas
While she was shrieking in the flame? Indeed,
By God, 'tis something beautifully wise
To be so circumspect.

SALADIN.   Come, come, forgive
Something to age. His lingerings cannot last.
He is not going to require of thee
First to turn jew.

TEMPLAR.   Who knows?

SALADIN.   Who? I, who know
This Nathan better.

TEMPLAR.   Yet the superstition
In which we have grown up, not therefore loses
When we detect it, all its influence on us.
Not all are free that can bemock their fetters.

SALADIN. Maturely said—but Nathan, surely Nathan—

TEMPLAR. The worst of superstitions is to think
One's own most bearable.

SALADIN.   May be, but Nathan—

TEMPLAR. Must Nathan be the mortal, who unshrinking
Can face the noon-tide ray of truth, nor there
Betray the twilight dungeon which he crawl'd from.

SALADIN. Yes, Nathan is that man.

TEMPLAR.   I thought so too,
But what if this pick'd man, this chosen sage,
Were such a thoro' jew, that he seeks out
For christian children to bring up as jews—
How then?

SALADIN.   Who says this of him?

TEMPLAR.   E'en the maid
With whom he frets me—with the hope of whom
He seem'd to joy in paying me the service,

Which he would not allow me to do gratis—
This very maid is not his daughter—no,
She is a kidnapp'd christian child.
    SALADIN.   Whom he
Has, notwithstanding, to thy wish refus'd?
    TEMPLAR *(with vehemence)*. Refus'd or not, I know him now.
There lies
The prating tolerationist unmask'd—
And I'll halloo upon this jewish wolf,
For all his philosophical sheep's-clothing,
Dogs that shall touze his hide.
    SALADIN *(earnestly)*.   Peace, christian!
    TEMPLAR.   What!
Peace, christian—and may jew and mussulman
Stickle for being jew and mussulman,
And must the christian only drop the christian?
    SALADIN *(more solemnly)*. Peace, christian!
    TEMPLAR *(calmly)*.   Yes, I feel what weight of blame
Lies in that word of thine pent up. O that
I knew how Assad in my place would act.
    SALADIN. He—not much better, probably as fiery.
Who has already taught thee thus at once
Like him to bribe me with a single word?
Indeed, if all has past as thou narratest,
I scarcely can discover Nathan in it.
But Nathan is my friend, and of my friends
One must not bicker with the other. Bend—
And be directed. Move with caution. Do not
Loose on him the fanatics of thy sect.
Conceal what all thy clergy would be claiming
My hand to avenge upon him, with more show
Of right than is my wish. Be not from spite
To any jew or mussulman a christian.
    TEMPLAR. Thy counsel is but on the brink of coming
Somewhat too late, thanks to the Patriarch's
Bloodthirsty rage, whose instrument I shudder
To have almost become.
    SALADIN.   How! how! thou wentest
Still earlier to the patriarch than to me?
    TEMPLAR. Yes, in the storm of passion, in the eddy
Of indecision—pardon—oh! thou wilt

No longer care, I fear, to find in me
One feature of thy Assad.
    SALADIN.   Yes, that fear.
Methinks I know by this time from what failings
Our virtue springs—this do thou cultivate,
Those shall but little harm thee in my sight
But go, seek Nathan, as he sought for thee,
And bring him hither: I must reconcile you.
If thou art serious about the maid—
Be calm, she shall be thine—Nathan shall feel
That without swine's flesh one may educate
A christian child, Go.   [*Templar withdraws.*
    SITTAH *(rising from the sofa).*   Very strange indeed!
    SALADIN. Well, Sittah, must my Assad not have been
A gallant handsome youth?
    SITTAH.   If he was thus,
And 'twasn't the Templar who sat to the painter.
But how cou'dst thou be so forgetful, brother,
As not to ask about his parents?
    SALADIN.   And
Particularly too about his mother.
Whether his mother e'er was in this country,
That is your meaning—isn't it?
    SITTAH.   You run on—
    SALADIN. Oh nothing is more possible, for Assad
'Mong handsome christian ladies was so welcome,
To handsome christian ladies so attached,
That once a report spread—but 'tis not pleasant
To bring that up. Let us be satisfied
That we have got him once again—have got him
With all the faults and freaks, the starts and wildness
Of his warm gentle heart—Oh, Nathan must
Give him the maid—Dost think so?
    SITTAH.   Give—give up!
    SALADIN. Aye, for what right has Nathan with the girl
If he be not her father? He who sav'd
Her life so lately has a stronger claim
To heir their rights who gave it her at first.
    SITTAH. What therefore, Saladin, if you withdraw
The maid at once from the unrightful owner?
    SALADIN. There is no need of that.

SITTAH.   Need, not precisely;
But female curiosity inspires
Me with that counsel. There are certain men
Of whom one is irresistibly impatient
To know what women they can be in love with.
    SALADIN. Well then you may send for her.
    SITTAH.   May I brother?
    SALADIN. But hurt not Nathan, he must not imagine
That we propose by violence to part them.
    SITTAH. Be without apprehension.
    SALADIN.   Fare you well,
I must make out where this Al-Hafi is.

SCENE.—*The Hall in Nathan's House, as in the first scene; the things there mentioned unpack'd and display'd.*

DAYA *and* NATHAN.

    DAYA. O how magnificent, how tasty, charming—
All such as only you could give—and where
Was this thin silver stuff with sprigs of gold
Woven? What might it cost? Yes, this is worthy
To be a wedding-garment. Not a queen
Could wish a handsomer.
    NATHAN.   Why wedding-garment?
    DAYA. Perhaps of that you thought not when you bought it;
But Nathan it must be so, must indeed.
It seems made for a bride—the pure white ground,
Emblem of innocence—the branching gold,
Emblem of wealth—Now is not it delightful?
    NATHAN. What's all this ingenuity of speech for?
Over whose wedding-gown are you displaying
Your emblematic learning? Have you found
A bridegroom?
    DAYA. I—
    NATHAN.   Who then?
    DAYA.   I—Gracious God!
    NATHAN. Who then? Whose wedding-garment do you speak
of?

For this is all your own and no one's else.

DAYA. Mine—is't for me and not for Recha?

NATHAN.   What
I brought for Recha is in another bale.
Come, clear it off; away with all your rubbish.

DAYA. You tempter—No—Were they the precious things
Of the whole universe, I will not touch them;
Until you promise me to seize upon
Such an occasion as heaven gives not twice.

NATHAN. Seize upon what occasion? For what end?

DAYA. There, do not act so strange. You must perceive
The Templar loves your Recha—Give her to him;
Then will your sin, which I can hide no longer,
Be at an end. The maid will come once more
Among the christians, will be once again
What she was born to, will be what she was;
And you, by all the benefits, for which
We cannot thank you enough, will not have heap'd
More coals of fire upon your head.

NATHAN.   Again
Harping on the old string, new tun'd indeed,
But so as neither to accord nor hold.

DAYA. How so?

NATHAN.   The templar pleases me indeed,
I 'd rather he than any one had Recha;
But—do have patience.

DAYA.   Patience—and is that
Not the old string you harp on?

NATHAN.   Patience, patience,
For a few days—no more. Ha! who comes here?
A friar—ask what he wants.

DAYA (going).   What can he want?

NATHAN. Give, give before he begs. O could I tell
How to come at the templar, not betraying
The motive of my curiosity—
For if I tell it, and if my suspicion
Be groundless, I have stak'd the father idly.
What is the matter?

DAYA (returning).   He must speak to you.

NATHAN. Then let him come to me. Go you meanwhile.
                    [Daya goes.

How gladly would I still remain my Recha's
Father. And can I not remain so, tho'
I cease to wear the name. To her, to her
I still shall wear it, when she once perceives
                                   [*Friar enters.*
How willingly I were so. Pious brother,
What can be done to serve you?

NATHAN and FRIAR.

FRIAR.   O not much;
And yet I do rejoice to see you yet
So well.
    NATHAN. You know me then—
    FRIAR.   Who knows you not?
You have impress'd your name in many a hand,
And it has been in mine these many years,
NATHAN *(feeling for his purse)*. Here, brother, I'll refresh it
    FRIAR.   Thank you, thank you
From poorer men I'd steal—but nothing now!
Only allow me to refresh my name
In your remembrance; for I too may boast
To have of old put something in your hand
Not to be scorn'd.
    NATHAN.   Excuse me I'm asham'd,
What was it? Claim it of me sevenfold,
I'm ready to atone for my forgetting.
    FRIAR. But before all, hear how this very day
I was reminded of the pledge I brought you.
    NATHAN. A pledge to me intrusted?
    FRIAR.   Some time since,
I dwelt as hermit on the Quarantana,
Not far from Jericho, but Arab robbers
Came and broke up my cell and oratory,
And dragg'd me with them. Fortunately I
Escap'd, and with the patriarch sought a refuge,
To beg of him some other still retreat,
Where I may serve my God in solitude
Until my latter end.
    NATHAN.   I stand on coals—
Quick, my good brother, let me know what pledge

You once intrusted to me.

FRIAR.   Presently,
Good Nathan, presently. The patriarch
Has promis'd me a hermitage on Thabor,
As soon as one is vacant, and meanwhile
Employs me as lay-brother in the convent,
And there I am at present: and I pine
A hundred times a day for Thabor; for
The patriarch will set me about all work,
And some that I can't brook—as for example—

NATHAN. Be speedy I beseech you.

FRIAR.   Now it happens
That some one whisper'd in his ear to-day,
There lives hard by a jew, who educates
A christian child as his own daughter.

NATHAN (startled).   How?

FRIAR. Hear me quite out. So he commissions me,
If possible to track him out this jew;
And storm'd most bitterly at the misdeed;
Which seems to him to be the very sin
Against the Holy Ghost—that is, the sin
Of all, most unforgiven, most enormous;
But luckily we cannot tell exactly
What it consists in—All at once my conscience
Was rous'd, and it occurr'd to me that I
Perhaps had given occasion to this sin.
Now do not you remember a knight's squire,
Who eighteen years ago gave to your hands
A female child a few weeks old?

NATHAN.   How that?
In fact such was—

FRIAR.   Now look with heed at me,
And recollect. I was the man on horseback
Who brought the child.

NATHAN.   Was you?

FRIAR.   And he, from whom
I brought it, was methinks a lord of Filnek—
Leonard of Filnek.

NATHAN.   Right!

FRIAR.   Because the mother

Died a short time before; and he, the father,
Had on a sudden to make off to Gazza,
Where the poor helpless thing could not go with him;
Therefore he sent it you—that was my message.
Did not I find you out at Darun? There
Consign it to you?

    NATHAN.   Yes.

    FRIAR.   It were no wonder
My memory deceiv'd me. I have had
Many a worthy master, and this one
I serv'd not long. He fell at Askalon—
But he was a kind lord.

    NATHAN.   O yes, indeed;
For much have I to thank him, very much—
He more than once preserv'd me from the sword.

    FRIAR. O brave—you therefore will with double pleasure
Have taken up this daughter.

    NATHAN.   You have said it.

    FRIAR. Where is she then? She is not dead I hope—
I would not have her dead, dear pretty creature.
If no one else know any thing about it
All is yet safe.

    NATHAN.   Aye all!

    FRIAR.   Yes, trust me, Nathan,
This is my way of thinking—if the good
That I propose to do is somehow twin'd
With mischief, then I let the good alone;
For we know pretty well what mischief is,
But not what's for the best. 'Twas natural
If you meant to bring up the christian child
Right well, that you should rear it as your own;
And to have done this lovingly and truly,
For such a recompense—were horrible.
It might have been more prudent to have had it
Brought up at second hand by some good christian
In her own faith. But your friend's orphan child
You would not then have lov'd. Children need love,
Were it the mute affection of a brute,
More at that age than christianity.
There's always time enough for that—and if
The maid have but grown up before your eyes

With a sound frame and pious—she remains
Still in her maker's eye the same. For is not
Christianity all built on judaism?
O, it has often vex'd me, cost me tears,
That christians will forget so often that
Our saviour was a jew.
   NATHAN.   You, my good brother,
Shall be my advocate, when bigot hate
And hard hypocrisy shall rise upon me—
And for a deed—a deed—thou, thou shalt know it—
But take it with thee to the tomb. As yet
Has vanity ne'er tempted me to tell it
To living soul—only to thee I tell it,
To simple piety alone; for it
Alone can feel what deeds the man who trusts
In God can gain upon himself.
   FRIAR.   You seem
Affected, and your eye-balls swim in water.
   NATHAN. 'Twas at Darun you met me with the child;
But you will not have known that a few days
Before, the christians murdered every jew in Gath,
Woman and child; that among these, my wife
With seven hopeful sons were found, who all
Beneath my brother's roof, which they had fled to,
Were burnt alive.
   FRIAR.   Just God!
   NATHAN.   And when you came,
Three nights had I in dust and ashes lain
Before my God and wept—aye, and at times
Arraign'd my maker, rag'd, and curs'd myself
And the whole world, and to christianity
Swore unrelenting hate.
   FRIAR.   Ah, I believe you.
   NATHAN. But by degrees returning reason came,
She spake with gentle voice—And yet God is,
And this was his decree—now exercise
What thou hast long imagin'd, and what surely
Is not more difficult to exercise
Than to imagine—if thou will it once.
I rose and call'd out—God, I will—I will,
So thou but aid my purpose—And behold

You was just then dismounted, and presented
To me the child wrapt in your mantle. What
You said, or I, occurs not to me now—
Thus much I recollect—I took the child,
I bore it to my couch, I kist it, flung
Myself upon my knees and sobbed—my God,
Now have I one out of the seven again!

    FRIAR. Nathan, you are a christian! Yes, by God
You are a christian—never was a better.

    NATHAN. Heaven bless us! What makes me to you a christian
Makes you to me a jew. But let us cease
To melt each other—time is nigh to act,
And tho' a sevenfold love had bound me soon
To this strange only girl, tho' the mere thought,
That I shall lose in her my seven sons
A second time, distracts me—yet I will,
If providence require her at my hands,
Obey.

    FRIAR.   The very thing I should advise you;
But your good genius has forestall'd my thought.

    NATHAN. The first best claimant must not seek to tear
Her from me.

    FRIAR.   No most surely not.

    NATHAN.   And he,
That has not stronger claims than I, at least
Ought to have earlier.

    FRIAR.   Certainly.

    NATHAN.   By nature
And blood conferr'd.

    FRIAR.   I mean so too.

    NATHAN.   Then name
The man allied to her as brother, uncle,
Or otherwise akin, and I from him
Will not withhold her—she who was created
And was brought up to be of any house,
Of any faith, the glory—I, I hope,
That of your master and his race you knew
More than myself.

    FRIAR.   I hardly think that, Nathan;
For I already told you that I pass'd
A short time with him.

NATHAN. Can you tell at least
The mother's family name? She was, I think,
A Stauffen.
FRIAR. May be—yes, in fact, you're right.
NATHAN. Conrade of Stauffen was her brother's name—
He was a templar.
FRIAR. I am clear it was.
But stay, I recollect I've yet a book,
'Twas my dead lord's—I drew it from his bosom,
While we were burying him at Askalon.
NATHAN. Well!
FRIAR. There are prayers in't, 'tis what we call
A breviary. This, thought I, may yet serve
Some christian man—not me indeed, for I
Can't read.
NATHAN. No matter, to the thing.
FRIAR. This book is written at both ends quite full,
And, as I'm told, contains, in his hand-writing,
About both him and her what's most material.
NATHAN. Go, run and fetch the book—'tis fortunate;
I am ready with its weight in gold to pay it,
And thousand thanks beside—Go, run.
FRIAR. Most gladly;
But 'tis in Arabic what he has written. [*Goes.*
NATHAN. No matter—that's all one—do fetch it—Oh!
If by its means I may retain the daughter,
And purchase with it such a son-in-law;
But that's unlikely—well, chance as it may.
Who now can have been with the patriarch
To tell this tale? That I must not forget
To ask about. If't were of Daya's?

NATHAN *and* DAYA.

DAYA *(anxiously breaks in).* Nathan!
NATHAN. Well!
DAYA. Only think, she was quite frightened at it,
Poor child, a message—
NATHAN. From the patriarch?
DAYA. No—
The sultan's sister, princess Sittah, sends.
NATHAN. And not the patriarch?

DAYA.   Can't you hear? The princess
Has sent to see your Recha.
    NATHAN.   Sent for Recha!
Has Sittah sent for Recha? Well if Sittah,
And not the patriarch, sends.
    DAYA.   Why think of him?
    NATHAN. Have you heard nothing from him lately—really
Seen nothing of him—whisper'd nothing to him?
    DAYA. How, I to him?
    NATHAN.   Where are the messengers?
    DAYA. There, just before you.
    NATHAN.   I will talk with them
Out of precaution. If there's nothing lurking
Beneath this message of the patriarch's doing—
                            [*Goes.*
    DAYA. And I—I've other fears. The only daughter,
As they suppose, of such a rich, rich jew,
Would for a mussulman be no bad thing;
I bet the templar will be chous'd, unless
I risk the second step, and to herself
Discover who she is. Let me for this
Employ the first short moments we're alone;
And that will be—oh, as I am going with her.
A serious hint upon the road I think
Can't be amiss—yes, now or never—yes.

ACT V.

SCENE.—*A Room in the Palace; the Purses still in a pile.*

SALADIN *and, soon after, several* MAMALUKES.

SALADIN *(as he comes in).* Here lies the money still, and no one finds
The dervis yet—he's probably got somewhere
Over a chess-board. Play would often make
The man forget himself, and why not, me.
Patience—Ha! what's the matter.

SALADIN *and* IBRAHIM.

IBRAHIM.   Happy news—
Joy, sultan, joy, the caravan from Cairo
Is safe arriv'd, and brings the seven years' tribute
Of the rich Nile.
SALADIN.   Bravo, my Ibrahim,
Thou always wast a welcome messenger,
And now at length—at length—accept my thanks
For the good tidings.
IBRAHIM *(waiting).*   Hither with them, sultan.
SALADIN. What art thou waiting for? Go.
IBRAHIM.   Nothing further
For my glad news?
SALADIN. What further?
IBRAHIM.   Errand boys
Earn hire—and when their message smiles i' the telling,
The sender's hire by the receiver's bounty
Is oft outweigh'd. Am I to be the first,
Whom Saladin at length has learnt to pay

89

In words? The first about whose recompense
The sultan higgled?

    SALADIN. Go, pick up a purse.

    IBRAHIM. No, not now—you might give them all away.

    SALADIN. All—hold, man. Here, come hither, take these two—
And is he really going—shall he conquer
Me then in generosity? for surely
'Tis harder for this fellow to refuse
Than 'tis for me to give. Here, Ibrahim—
Shall I be tempted, just before my exit,
To be a different man—shall Saladin
Not die like Saladin, then wherefore live so?

ABDALLAH *and* SALADIN.

    ABDALLAH. Hail, Sultan!

    SALADIN.   If thou comest to inform me
That the whole convoy is arrived from Egypt,
I know it already.

    ABDALLAH.   Do I come too late?

    SALADIN. Too late, and why too late? There for thy tidings
Pick up a purse or two.

    ABDLLAH.   Does that make three?

    SALADIN. So thou wouldst reckon—well, well, take them, take
them.

    ABDALLAH. A third will yet be here if he be able.

    SALADIN. How so?

    ABDALLAH.   He may perhaps have broke his neck.
We three, as soon as certain of the coming
Of the rich caravan, each crost our horses,
And gallop'd hitherward. The foremost fell,
Then I was foremost, and continued so
Into the city, but sly Ibrahim,
Who knows the streets—

    SALADIN.   But he that fell, go, seek him.

    IBDALLAH. That will I quickly—if he lives, the half
Of what I've got is his.   [*Goes.*

    SALADIN.   What a fine fellow!
And who can boast such mamalukes as these;
And is it not allowed me to imagine
That my example help'd to form them. Hence
With the vile thought at last to turn another.

A third COURIER.

Sultan—
    SALADIN. Was't thou who fell?
    COURIER.   No, I've to tell thee
That Emir Mansor, who conducts the convoy,
Alights.
    SALADIN.   O bring him to me—Ah, he's there—
Be welcome, Emir. What has happen'd to thee?
For we have long expected thee.

SALADIN *and* EMIR.

    EMIR *(after the wont obeisance).*   This letter
Will show, that, in Thebais, discontents
Requir'd thy Abulkassem's sabred hand,
Ere we could march. Since that, our progress, sultan,
My zeal has sped most anxiously.
    SALADIN.   I trust thee—
But my good Mansor take without delay—
Thou art not loth to go further—fresh protection,
And with the treasure on to Libanon;
The greater part at least I have to lodge
With my old father.
    EMIR.   O, most willingly.
    SALADIN. And take not a slight escort Libanon
Is far from quiet, as thou wilt have heard;
The templars stir afresh, be therefore cautious.
Come, I must see thy troop, and give the orders.
                      [To a slave.
Say I shall be with Sittah when I've finish'd.

SCENE.—*A Place of Palms.*

The TEMPLAR *walking to and fro.*

    TEMPLAR. Into this house I go not—sure at last
He'll show himself—once, once they us'd to see me
So instantly, so gladly—time will come
When he'll send out most civilly to beg me
Not to pace up and down before his door.
Psha—and yet I'm a little nettled too;

And what has thus embitter'd me against him?
He answered yes. He has refus'd me nothing
As yet. And Saladin has undertaken
To bring him round. And does the christian nestle
Deeper in me than the jew lurks in him?
Who, who can justly estimate himself?
How comes it else that I should grudge him so
The little booty that he took such pains
To rob the christians of? A theft, no less
Than such a creature tho'— but whose, whose creature?
Sure not the slave's who floated the mere block
On to life's barren strand, and then ran off;
But his the artist's, whose fine fancy moulded
Upon the unown'd block a godlike form,
Whose chisel grav'd it there. Recha's true father,
Spite of the christian who begot her, is,
Must ever be, the jew. Alas, were I
To fancy her a simple christian wench,
And without all that which the jew has given,
Which only such a jew could have bestow'd—
Speak out my heart, what had she that would please thee?
No, nothing! Little! For her very smile
Shrinks to a pretty twisting of the muscles—
Be that, which makes her smile, suppos'd unworthy
Of all the charms in ambush on her lips?
No, not her very smile—I've seen sweet smiles
Spent on conceit, on foppery, on slander,
On flatterers, on wicked wooers spent,
And did they charm me then? then wake the wish
To flutter out a life beneath their sunshine?
Indeed not—Yet I'm angry with the man
Who alone gave this higher value to her.
How this, and why? Do I deserve the taunt
With which I was dismiss'd by Saladin?
'Tis bad enough that Saladin should think so;
How little, how contemptible must I
Then have appear'd to him—all for a girl.
Conrade, this will not do—back, back—And if
Daya to boot had prated matter to me
Not easy to be proved—At last he's coming,
Engag'd in earnest converse—and with whom?

My friar in Nathan's house! then he knows all—
Perhaps has to the patriarch been betray'd.
O Conrade, what vile mischiefs thou hast brooded
Out of thy cross-grain'd head, that thus one spark
Of that same passion, love, can set so much
O' th' brain in flame? Quick then, determine, wretch,
What shalt thou say or do? Step back a moment
And see if this good friar will please to quit him.

> NATHAN *and the* FRIAR *come together out of Nathan's house.*

NATHAN. Once more, good brother, thanks.
FRIAR.   The like to you.
NATHAN. To me, and why; because I'm obstinate—
Would force upon you what you have no use for?
FRIAR. The book besides was none of mine. Indeed
It must at any rate belong to th' daughter;
It is her whole, her only patrimony—
Save she has you. God grant you ne'er have reason
To sorrow for the much you've done for her.
NATHAN. How should I? that can never be; fear nothing.
FRIAR. Patriarchs and templars—
NATHAN.   Have not in their power
Evil enough to make me e'er repent.
And then—But are you really well assured
It is a templar who eggs on your patriarch?
FRIAR. It scarcely can be other, for a templar
Talk'd with him just before, and what I heard
Agreed with this.
NATHAN.   But there is only one
Now in Jerusalem; and him I know;
He is my friend, a noble open youth.
FRIAR. The same. But what one is at heart, and what
One gets to be in active life, mayn't always
Square well together.
NATHAN.   No, alas, they do not.
Therefore unanger'd I let others do
Their best or worst. O brother, with your book
I set all at defiance, and am going
Strait with it to the sultan.
FRIAR.   God be with you!
Here I shall take my leave.

NATHAN.   And have not seen her—
Come soon, come often to us. If to-day
The patriarch make out nothing—but no matter,
Tell him it all to-day, or when you will.
    FRIAR. Not I—farewell!
    NATHAN.   Do not forget us, brother.
My God, why may I not beneath thy sky
Here drop upon my knees; now the twin'd knot,
Which has so often made my thinkings anxious,
Untangles of itself—God, how I am eased,
Now that I've nothing in the world remaining
That I need hide—now that I can as freely
Walk before man as before thee, who only
Need'st not to judge a creature by his deeds—
Deeds which so seldom are his own—O God!

NATHAN and TEMPLAR.

TEMPLAR (*coming forward*).
Hoa, Nathan, take me with you.
    NATHAN.   Ha! Who calls?
Is it you, knight? And whither have you been
That you could not be met with at the sultan's?
    TEMPLAR. We miss'd each other—take it not amiss.
    NATHAN. I, no, but Saladin.
    TEMPLAR.   You was just gone.
    NATHAN. O, then you spoke with him; I'm satisfied.
    TEMPLAR. Yes—but he wants to talk with us together.
    NATHAN. So much the better. Come with me, my step
Was eitherwise bent thither.
    TEMPLAR.   May I ask,
Nathan, who 'twas now left you?
    NATHAN.   Did you know him?
    TEMPLAR. Was't that good-hearted creature the lay-brother,
Whom the hoar patriarch has a knack of using
To feel his way out?
    NATHAN.   That may be. In fact
He's at the patriarch's.
    TEMPLAR.   'Tis no awkward hit
To make simplicity the harbinger
Of craft.
    NATHAN.   If the simplicity of dunces,

But if of honest piety?
 TEMPLAR.   This last
No patriarch can believe in.
 NATHAN.   I'll be bound for't
This last belongs to him who quitted me,
He'll not assist his patriarch to accomplish
A vile or cruel purpose.
 TEMPLAR.   Such, at least,
He would appear—but has he told you then
Something of me?
 NATHAN.   Of you? No—not by name,
He can't well be acquainted with your name.
 TEMPLAR. No, that not.
 NATHAN.   He indeed spoke of a templar,
Who—
 TEMPLAR. What?
 NATHAN.   But by this templar could not mean
To point out you.
 TEMPLAR.   Stay, stay, who knows? Let's hear.
 NATHAN. Who has accus'd me to his patriarch.
 TEMPLAR. Accus'd thee, no, that by his leave is false.
Nathan, do hear me—I am not the man
Who would deny a single of his actions;
What I have done, I did. Nor am I one
Who would defend all he has done as right—
Why be asham'd of failing? Am I not
Firmly resolv'd on better future conduct?
And am I not aware how much the man
That's willing can improve? O, hear me, Nathan—
I am the templar your lay-brother talk'd of—
Who has accus'd—You know what made me angry,
What set the blood in all my veins on fire,
The mad-cap that I was—I had drawn nigh
To fling myself with soul and body whole
Into your arms—and you receiv'd me, Nathan—
How cold, how luke-warm, for that's worse than cold.—
How, with words weigh'd and measur'd, you took care
To put me off; and with what questioning
About my parentage, and God knows what,
You seem'd to answer me—I must not think on't
If I would keep my temper—Hear me, Nathan—

While in this ferment—Daya steps behind me,
Bolts out a secret in my ear, which seem'd
At once to lend the clue to your behavior.
    NATHAN. How so?
    TEMPLAR.   Do hear me to the end. I fancy'd
That what you from the christians had purloin'd
You wasn't content to let a christian have;
And so the project struck me short and good,
To hold the knife to your throat till—
    NATHAN.   Short and good;
And good—but where's the good?
    TEMPLAR. Yet hear me, Nathan,
I own I did not right—you are unguilty,
No doubt. The prating Daya does not know
What she reported—has a grudge against you—
Seeks to involve you in an ugly business—
May be, may be, and I'm a crazy looby,
A credulous enthusiast—both ways mad—
Doing ever much too much, or much too little—
That too may be—forgive me, Nathan.
    NATHAN.   If
Such be the light in which you view—
    TEMPLAR.   In short
I to the patriarch went. I nam'd you not
That, as I said, was false. I only stated
In general terms, the case, to learn his notion,
That too might have been let alone—assuredly.
For knew I not the patriarch then to be
A knave? And might I not have talk'd with you?
And ought I to have expos'd the poor girl—ha!
To part with such a father? Now what happens?
The patriarch's villainy consistent ever
Restor'd me to myself—O, hear me out—
Suppose he was to ferret out your name,
What then? What then? He cannot seize the maid,
Unless she still belong to none but you.
'Tis from your house alone that he could drag her
Into a convent; therefore, grant her me—
Grant her to me, and let him come. By God—
Sever my wife from me—he'll not be rash
Enough to think about it. Give her to me,

Be she or no thy daughter, christian, jewess,
Or neither, 'tis all one, all one—I'll never
In my whole life ask of thee which she is,
Be't as it may.

NATHAN.   You may perhaps imagine
That I've an interest to conceal the truth.

TEMPLAR. Be't as it may.

NATHAN.   I neither have to you
Nor any one, whom it behooved to know it,
Denied that she's a christian, and no more
Than my adopted daughter. Why, to her
I have not yet betray'd it—I am bound
To justify only to her.

TEMPLAR.   Of that
Shall be no need. Indulge, indulge her with
Never beholding you with other eyes—
Spare, spare her the discovery. As yet
You have her to yourself, and may bestow her;
Give her to me—oh, I beseech thee Nathan,
Give her to me, I, only I can save her
A second time, and will.

NATHAN.   Yes, could have sav'd her,
But 'tis all over now—it is too late.

TEMPLAR. How so, too late.

NATHAN.   Thanks to the patriarch.

TEMPLAR.   How,
Thanks to the patriarch, and for what? Can he
Earn thanks of us. For what?

NATHAN.   That now we know
To whom she is related—to whose hands
She may with confidence be now delivered.

TEMPLAR. He thank him who has more to thank him for.

NATHAN. From theirs you now have to obtain her, not
From mine.

TEMPLAR.   Poor Recha—what befalls thee? Oh,
Poor Recha—what had been to other orphans
A blessing, is to thee a curse. But, Nathan,
Where are they, these new kinsmen?

NATHAN.   Where they are?

TEMPLAR. Who are they?
                    Who—a brother is found out

To whom you must address yourself.

TEMPLAR.   A brother!
And what is he, a soldier or a priest?
Let's hear what I've to hope.

NATHAN.   As I believe
He's neither of the two—or both. Just now
I cannot say exactly.

TEMPLAR.   And besides
He's—

NATHAN.   A brave follow, and with whom my
Recha
Will not be badly placed.

TEMPLAR.   But he's a christian.
At times I know not what to make of you—
Take it not ill of me, good Nathan. Will she
Not have to play the christian among christians;
And when she has been long enough the actress
Not turn so? Will the tares in time not stifle
The pure wheat of your setting—and does that
Affect you not a whit—you yet declare
She'll not be badly plac'd.

NATHAN.   I think, I hope so.
And should she there have need of any thing
Has she not you and me?

TEMPLAR.   Need at her brother's—
What should she need when there? Won't he provide
His dear new sister with all sorts of dresses,
With comfits and with toys and glittering jewels?
And what needs any sister wish for else—
Only a husband? And he comes in time.
A brother will know how to furnish that,
The christianer the better. Nathan, Nathan,
O what an angel you had form'd, and how
Others will mar it now!

NATHAN.   Be not so downcast,
Believe me he will ever keep himself
Worthy our love.

TEMPLAR.   No, say not that of mine.
My love allows of no refusal—none.
Were it the merest trifle—but a name.
Hold there—has she as yet the least suspicion

Of what is going forward?

NATHAN.   That may be,
And yet I know not whence.

TEMPLAR.   It matters not,
She shall, she must in either case from me
First learn what fate is threatening. My fixt purpose
To see her not again, nor speak to her,
Till I might call her mine, is gone. I hasten—

NATHAN. Stay, whither would you go?

TEMPLAR.   To her, to learn
If this girl's soul be masculine enough
To form the only resolution worthy
Herself.

NATHAN. What resolution?

TEMPLAR. This—to ask
No more about her brother and her father,
And—

NATHAN.   And—

TEMPLAR.   To follow me. E'en if she were
Bo doing to become a moslem's wife.

NATHAN. Stay, you'll not find her—she is now with Sittah,
The Sultan's sister.

TEMPLAR.   How long since, and wherefore?

NATHAN. And would you there behold her brother, come
Thither with me.

TEMPLAR.   Her brother, whose then? Sittah's
Or Recha's do you mean?

NATHAN.   Both, both, perchance.
Come this way—I beseech you, come with me.

                    [*Leads off the Templar with him.*

SCENE.—*The Sultan's Palace. A Room in Sittah's Apartment*

SITTAH *and* RECHA.

SITTAH. How I am pleas'd with thee, sweet girl! But do
Shake off this perturbation, be not anxious,
Be not alarm'd, I want to hear thee talk—
Be cheerful.

RECHA. Princess!

SITTAH. No, not princess, child,
Call me thy friend, or Sittah, or thy sister,
Or rather aunt, for I might well be thine;
So young, so good, so prudent, so much knowledge,
You must have read a great deal to be thus.

RECHA. I read—you're laughing, Sittah, at your sister,
I scarce can read.

SITTAH. Scarce can, you little fibber.

RECHA. My father's hand or so—I thought you spoke
Of books.

SITTAH. Aye, surely so I did, of books.

RECHA. Well really now it puzzles me to read them.

SITTAH. In earnest?

RECHA. Yes, in earnest, for my father
Hates cold book-learning, which makes an impression
With its dead letters only on the brain.

SITTAH. What say you? Aye, he's not unright in that
So then the greater part of what you know—

RECHA. I know but from his mouth—of most of it
I could relate to you, the how, the where,
The why he taught it me.

SITTAH. So it clings closer,
And the whole soul drinks in th' instruction.

RECHA. Yes,
And Sittah certainly has not read much.

SITTAH. How so? Not that I'm vain of having read;
But what can be thy reason? Speak out boldly,
Thy reason for it.

RECHA. She is so right down,
Unartificial—only like herself,
And books do seldom leave us so; my father
Says.

SITTAH. What a man thy father is, my Recha.

RECHA. Is not he?

SITTAH. How he always hits the mark.

RECHA. Does not he? And this father—

SITTAH. Love, what ails thee?

RECHA. This father—

SITTAH. God, thou'rt weeping!

RECHA. And this father—

It must have vent, my heart wants room, wants room.
SITTAH. Child, child, what ails you, Recha?
    RECHA.   And this father
I am to lose.
    SITTAH.   Thou lose him, O no, never:
Arise, be calm, how so? It must not be.
    RECHA. So shall thy offer not have been in vain,
To be my friend, my sister.
    SITTAH.   Maid, I am.
Rise then, or I must call for help.
    RECHA.   Forgive,
My agony made me awhile forgetful
With whom I am. Tears, sobbing, and despair,
Can not avail with Sittah. Cool calm reason
Alone is over her omnipotent;
Whose cause that pleads before her, he has conquer'd.
    SITTAH. Well then!
    RECHA.   My friend, my sister, suffer not
Another father to be forc'd upon me.
    SITTAH. Another father to be forc'd upon thee—
Who can do that, or wish to do it, Recha?
    RECHA. Who? Why my good, my evil genius, Daya,
She, she can wish it, will it—and can do it.
You do not know this dear good evil Daya.
God, God forgive it her—reward her for it;
So much good she has done me, so much evil.
    SITTAH. Evil to thee—much goodness she can't have.
    RECHA. O yes, she has indeed.
    SITTAH.   Who is she?
    RECHA.   Who?
A christian, who took care of all my childhood.
You cannot think how little she allow'd me
To miss a mother—God reward her for it—
But then she has so teas'd, so tortur'd me.
    SITTAH. And about what? Why, how, when?
    RECHA.   The poor woman,
I tell thee, is a christian—and she must
From love torment—is one of those enthusiasts
Who think they only know the one true road
To God.
    SITTAH.   I comprehend thee.

RECHA.   And who feel
Themselves in duty bound to point it out
To every one who is not in this path,
To lead, to drag them into it. And indeed
They can't do otherwise consistently;
For if theirs really be the only road
On which 'tis safe to travel—they cannot
With comfort see their friends upon another
Which leads to ruin, to eternal ruin:
Else were it possible at the same instant
To love and hate the same man. Nor is 't this
Which forces me to be aloud complainant.
Her groans, her prayers, her warnings, and her threats,
I willingly should have abided longer—
Most willingly—they always called up thoughts
Useful and good; and whom does it not flatter
To be by whomsoever held so dear,
So precious, that they cannot bear the thought
Of parting with us at some time for ever?
    SITTAH. Most true.
    RECHA.   But—but—at last this goes too far;
I've nothing to oppose to it, neither patience,
Neither reflection—nothing.
    SITTAH.   How, to what?
    RECHA. To what she has just now, as she will have it,
Discover'd to me.
    SITTAH.   How discover'd to thee?
    RECHA. Yes, just this instant. Coming hitherward
We past a fallen temple of the christians—
She all at once stood still, seem'd inly struggling,
Turn'd her moist eyes to heaven, and then on me.
Come, says she finally, let us to the right
Thro' this old fane—she leads the way, I follow.
My eyes with horror overran the dim
And tottering ruin—all at once she stops
By the sunk steps of a low moorish altar.—
O how I felt, when there, with streaming tears
And wringing hands, prostrate before my feet
She fell.
    SITTAH.   Good child—
    RECHA.   And by the holy virgin,

Who there had hearken'd many a prayer, and wrought
Many a wonder, she conjur'd, intreated,
With looks of heartfelt sympathy and love,
I would at length take pity of myself—
At least forgive, if she must now unfold
What claims her church had on me.
    SITTAH.   Ah! I guess'd it.
    RECHA. That I am sprung of Christian blood—baptiz'd—
Not Nathan's daughter—and he not my father.
God, God, he not my father! Sittah, Sittah,
See me once more low at thy feet
    SITTAH.   O Recha,
Not so; arise, my brother's coming, rise.

SALADIN, SITTAH, *and* RECHA.

    SALADIN *(entering)*. What is the matter Sittah?
    SITTAH.   She is swoon'd—
God—
    SALADIN.   Who?
    SITTAH.   You know sure.
    SALADIN.   What our Nathan's daughter?
What ails her?
    SITTAH.   Child, come to thyself, the sultan.
    RECHA. No, I'll not rise, not rise, not look upon
The sultan's countenance—I'll not admire
The bright reflection of eternal justice
And mercy on his brow, and in his eye,
Before—
    SALADIN.   Rise, rise.
    RECHA.   Before he shall have promis'd—
    SALADIN. Come, come, I promise whatsoe'er thy prayer.
    RECHA. Nor more nor less than leave my father to me,
And me to him. As yet I cannot tell
What other wants to be my father. Who
Can want it, care I not to enquire. Does blood
Alone then make the father? blood alone?
    SALADIN *(raising her)*. Who was so cruel in thy breast to shed
This wild suspicion? Is it prov'd, made clear?
    RECHA. It must, for Daya had it from my nurse,
Whose dying lips intrusted it to her.
    SALADIN. Dying, perhaps delirious; if 'twere true,

Blood only does not make by much the father,
Scarcely the father of a brute, scarce gives
The first right to endeavour at deserving
The name of father. If there be two fathers
At strive for thee, quit both, and take a third,
And take me for thy father.

SITTAH.   Do it, do it.

SALADIN. I will be a kind father—but methinks
A better thought occurs, what hast thou need
Of father upon father? They will die,
So that 'tis better to look out by times
For one that starts fair, and stakes life with life
On equal terms. Knowst thou none such?

SITTAH.   My brother,
Don't make her blush.

SALADIN.   Why that was half my project.
Blushing so well becomes the ugly, that
The fair it must make charming—I have order'd
Thy father Nathan hither, and another,
Dost guess who 'tis? one other.—Sittah, you
Will not object?

SITTAH.   Brother—

SALADIN.   And when he comes,
Sweet girl, then blush to crimson.

RECHA.   Before whom—
Blush?

SALADIN.   Little hypocrite—or else grow pale,
Just as thou willst and canst. Already there?

SITTAH (*to a female slave who comes in*).
Well, be they usher'd in. Brother, 'tis they.

SALADIN, SITTAH, RECHA, NATHAN, *and* TEMPLAR.

SALADIN. Welcome my dear good friends. Nathan, to you
I've first to mention, you may send and fetch
Your monies when you will.

NATHAN.   Sultan—

SALADIN.   And now
I'm at your service.

NATHAN.   Sultan—

SALADIN.   For my treasures
Are all arriv'd. The caravan is safe.

I'm richer than I've been these many years.
Now tell me what you wish for, to achieve
Some splendid speculation—you in trade
Like us, have never too much ready cash.

    NATHAN *(going towards Recha).* Why first about this trifle?—I behold
An eye in tears, which 'tis far more important
To me to dry. My Recha thou hast wept,
What hast thou lost? Thou art still, I trust, my daughter.

    RECHA. My father!

    NATHAN.   That's enough, we are understood
By one another; but be calm, be cheerful.
If else thy heart be yet thy own—if else
No threaten'd loss thy trembling bosom wring—
Thy father shall remain to thee.

    RECHA.   None, none.

    TEMPLAR. None, none—then I'm deceiv'd. What we don't fear
To lose, we never fancied, never wish'd
Ourselves possess'd of. But 'tis well, 'tis well.
Nathan, this changes all—all. Saladin,
At thy command we came, but I misled thee,
Trouble thyself no further.

    SALADIN.   Always headlong;
Young man, must every will then bow to thine,
Interpret all thy meanings?

    TEMPLAR.   Thou hast heard,
Sultan, hast seen.

    SALADIN.   Aye, 'twas a little awkward
Not to be certain of thy cause.

    TEMPLAR.   I now
Do know my doom.

    SALADIN.   Pride in an act of service
Revokes the benefit. What thou hast sav'd
Is therefore not thy own, or else the robber,
Urg'd by his avarice thro' fire-crumbling halls,
Were like thyself a hero. Come, sweet maid,

                    [*Advances toward Recha in order to
lead her up to the templar.*
Come, stickle not for niceties with him.
Other—he were less warm and proud, and had

Paus'd, and not sav'd thee. Balance then the one
Against the other, and put him to the blush,
Do what he should have done—own thou thy love—
Make him thy offer, and if he refuse,
Or e'er forgot how infinitely more
By this thou do for him than he for thee—
What, what in fact has he then done for thee
But make himself a little sooty? That
(Else he has nothing of my Assad in him,
But only wears his mask) that was mere sport.
Come lovely girl.

    SITTAH.   Go, go, my love, this step
Is for thy gratitude too short, too trifling.
[*They are each taking one of Recha's hands when Nathan with a solemn
gesture of prohibition says,*

    NATHAN. Hold, Saladin—hold, Sittah.
    SALADIN.   Ha! thou too? Nathan.
    NATHAN.   One other has to speak.
    SALADIN.   Who denies that?
Unquestionably, Nathan, there belongs
A vote to such a foster-father—and
The first, if you require it. You perceive
I know how all the matter lies.

    NATHAN.   Not all—
I speak not of myself. There is another,
A very different man, whom, Saladin,
I must first talk with.

    SALADIN.   Who?
    NATHAN.   Her brother.
    SALADIN.   Recha's?
    NATHAN. Yes, hers.
    RECHA.   My brother—have I then a brother?
[*The templar starts from his silent and sullen inattention.*

    TEMPLAR. Where is this brother? Not yet here? 'Twas here
I was to find him.

    NATHAN. Patience yet awhile.

    TEMPLAR (*very bitterly*). He has impos'd a father on the girl,
He'll find her up a brother.

    SALADIN.   That was wanting!
Christian, this mean suspicion ne'er had past
The lips of Assad. Go but on—

NATHAN.   Forgive him,
I can forgive him readily. Who knows
What in his place, and at his time of life,
We might have thought ourselves? Suspicion, knight,
                    [*Approaching the templar in a friendly*
manner.
Succeeds soon to mistrust. Had you at first
Favor'd me with your real name.
　　TEMPLAR.   How? what?
　　NATHAN. You are no Stauffen.
　　TEMPLAR.   Who then am I? Speak.
　　NATHAN. Conrade of Stauffen is no name of yours.
　　TEMPLAR. What is my name then?
　　NATHAN.   Guy of Filnek.
　　TEMPLAR.   How?
　　NATHAN. You startle—
　　TEMPLAR.   And with reason. Who says that?
　　NATHAN. I, who can tell you more. Meanwhile, observe
I do not tax you with a falsehood.
　　TEMPLAR.   No?
　　NATHAN. May be you with propriety can wear
Yon name as well.
　　TEMPLAR.   I think so too. (God—God
Put that speech on his tongue.)
　　NATHAN.   In fact your mother –
She was a Stauffen: and her brother's name,
(The uncle to whose care you were resigned,
When by the rigor of the climate chas'd,
Your parents quitted Germany to seek
This land once more) was Conrade. He perhaps
Adopted you as his own son and heir.
Is it long since you hither travell'd with him?
Is he alive yet?
　　TEMPLAR.   So in fact it stands.
What shall I say? Yes, Nathan, 'tis all right:
Tho' he himself is dead. I came to Syria
With the last reinforcement of our order,
But—but what has all this long tale to do
With Recha's brother, whom—
　　NATHAN.   Your father—
　　TEMPLAR.   Him,

Him did you know?

    NATHAN. He was my friend.

    TEMPLAR.   Your friend?

And is that possible?

    NATHAN.   He called himself

Leonard of Filnek, but he was no German.

    TEMPLAR. You know that too?

    NATHAN.   He had espous'd a German,

And followed for a time your mother thither.

    TEMPLAR. No more I beg of you—But Recha's brother—

    NATHAN. Art thou!

    TEMPLAR. I, I her brother—

    RECHA.   He, my brother?

    SITTAH. So near akin—

    RECHA *(offers to clasp him)*. My brother!

    TEMPLAR *(steps back)*.   Brother to her—

    RECHA *(turning to Nathan)*. It cannot be, his heart knows

nothing of it

We are deceivers, God.

    SALADIN *(to the templar)*.   Deceivers, yes:

All is deceit in thee, face, voice, walk, gesture,

Nothing belongs to thee. How, not acknowledge

A sister such as she? Go.

    TEMPLAR *(modestly approaching him)*.   Sultan, sultan,

O do not misinterpret my amazement—

Thou never saw'st in such a moment, prince,

Thy Assad's heart—mistake not him and me.

                      [*Hastening towards Nathan.*

O Nathan, you have taken, you have given,

Both with full hands indeed; and now—yes—yes,

You give me more than you have taken from me,

Yes, infinitely more—my sister—sister.

                      [*Embraces Recha.*

    NATHAN. Blanda of Filnek.

    TEMPLAR.   Blanda, ha! not Recha,

Your Recha now no longer—you resign her,

Give her her christian name again, and then

For my sake turn her off. Why Nathan, Nathan,

Why must she suffer for it? she for me?

    NATHAN. What mean you? O my children, both my children—

For sure my daughter's brother is my child,

So soon as he but will it.   *[While they embrace Nathan by turns, Saladin draws nigh to Sittah.*

SALADIN.   What sayst thou
Sittah to this?

SITTAH.   I'm deeply mov'd.

SALADIN.   And I
Half tremble at the thought of the emotion
Still greater, still to come. Nathan, a word
                    *[While he converses with Nathan,
Sittah goes to express her sympathy to the others.*
With thee apart. Wast thou not saying also
That her own father was no German born?
What was he then? Whence was he?

NATHAN.   He himself
Never intrusted me with that. From him
I knew it not.

SALADIN.   You say he was no Frank?

NATHAN. No, that he own'd: he loved to talk the Persian.

SALADIN. The Persian—need I more? 'Tis he—'twas he!

NATHAN. Who?

SALADIN.   Assad certainly, my brother Assad.

NATHAN. If thou thyself perceive it, be assur'd;
Look in this book—   *[Gives the breviary.*

SALADIN *(eagerly looking).*   O 'tis his hand, his hand,
I recollect it well.

NATHAN.   They know it not;
It rests with thee what they shall learn of this.

SALADIN *(turning over the breviary).* I not acknowledge my own
brother's children,
Not own my nephew—not my children—I
Leave them to thee? Yes, Sittah, it is they, *[Aloud.*
They are my brother's and thy brother's children.
                    [Rushes to embrace them.

SITTAH. What do I hear? Could it be otherwise? *[The like.*

SALADIN *(to the templar).* Now, proud boy, thou shalt love me,
thou must love me,
                    [To Recha.
And I am, what I offer'd to become,
With or without thy leave.

SITTAH.   I too—I too.

SALADIN *(to the templar).* My son—my Assad—my lost Assad's son.

TEMPLAR. I of thy blood—then those were more than dreams
With which they us'd to lull my infancy—
Much more.   [*Falls at the sultan's feet.*

    SALADIN *(raising him).* Now mark his malice. Something of it
He knew, yet would have let me butcher him—
Boy, boy!   [*During the silent continuance of
reciprocal embraces the curtain falls.*

POETRY

101 GREAT AMERICAN POEMS, Edited by The American Poetry & Literacy Project. (0-486-40158-8)

100 BEST-LOVED POEMS, Edited by Philip Smith. (0-486-28553-7)

ENGLISH ROMANTIC POETRY: An Anthology, Edited by Stanley Appelbaum. (0-486-29282-7)

THE INFERNO, Dante Alighieri. Translated and with notes by Henry Wadsworth Longfellow. (0-486-44288-8)

PARADISE LOST, John Milton. Introduction and Notes by John A. Himes. (0-486-44287-X)

SPOON RIVER ANTHOLOGY, Edgar Lee Masters. (0-486-27275-3)

SELECTED CANTERBURY TALES, Geoffrey Chaucer. (0-486-28241-4)

SELECTED POEMS, Emily Dickinson. (0-486-26466-1)

LEAVES OF GRASS: The Original 1855 Edition, Walt Whitman. (0-486-45676-5)

COMPLETE SONNETS, William Shakespeare. (0-486-26686-9)

THE RAVEN AND OTHER FAVORITE POEMS, Edgar Allan Poe. (0-486-26685-0)

ENGLISH VICTORIAN POETRY: An Anthology, Edited by Paul Negri. (0-486-40425-0)

SELECTED POEMS, Walt Whitman. (0-486-26878-0)

THE ROAD NOT TAKEN AND OTHER POEMS, Robert Frost. (0-486-27550-7)

AFRICAN-AMERICAN POETRY: An Anthology, 1773-1927, Edited by Joan R. Sherman. (0-486-29604-0)

GREAT SHORT POEMS, Edited by Paul Negri. (0-486-41105-2)

THE RIME OF THE ANCIENT MARINER, Samuel Taylor Coleridge. (0-486-27266-4)

THE WASTE LAND, PRUFROCK AND OTHER POEMS, T. S. Eliot. (0-486-40061-1)

SONG OF MYSELF, Walt Whitman. (0-486-41410-8)

AENEID, Vergil. (0-486-28749-1)

SONGS FOR THE OPEN ROAD: Poems of Travel and Adventure, Edited by The American Poetry & Literacy Project. (0-486-40646-6)

SONGS OF INNOCENCE AND SONGS OF EXPERIENCE, William Blake. (0-486-27051-3)

WORLD WAR ONE BRITISH POETS: Brooke, Owen, Sassoon, Rosenberg and Others, Edited by Candace Ward. (0-486-29568-0)

GREAT SONNETS, Edited by Paul Negri. (0-486-28052-7)

CHRISTMAS CAROLS: Complete Verses, Edited by Shane Weller. (0-486-27397-0)

PLAYS

THE TAMING OF THE SHREW, William Shakespeare. (0-486-29765-9)

MACBETH, William Shakespeare. (0-486-27802-6)

KING LEAR, William Shakespeare. (0-486-28058-6)

FOUR GREAT HISTORIES: Henry IV Part I, Henry IV Part II, Henry V, and Richard III, William Shakespeare. (0-486-44629-8)

THE TEMPEST, William Shakespeare. (0-486-40658-X)

JULIUS CAESAR, William Shakespeare. (0-486-26876-4)

TWELFTH NIGHT; OR, WHAT YOU WILL, William Shakespeare. (0-486-29290-8)

HEARTBREAK HOUSE, George Bernard Shaw. (0-486-29291-6)

PYGMALION, George Bernard Shaw. (0-486-28222-8)

ARMS AND THE MAN, George Bernard Shaw. (0-486-26476-9)

OEDIPUS REX, Sophocles. (0-486-26877-2)

ANTIGONE, Sophocles. (0-486-27804-2)

FIVE GREAT GREEK TRAGEDIES, Sophocles, Euripides and Aeschylus. (0-486-43620-9)

THE FATHER, August Strindberg. (0-486-43217-3)

THE PLAYBOY OF THE WESTERN WORLD AND RIDERS TO THE SEA, J. M. Synge. (0-486-27562-0)

TWELVE CLASSIC ONE-ACT PLAYS, Edited by Mary Carolyn Waldrep. (0-486-47490-9)

LADY WINDERMERE'S FAN, Oscar Wilde. (0-486-40078-6)

AN IDEAL HUSBAND, Oscar Wilde. (0-486-41423-X)

THE IMPORTANCE OF BEING EARNEST, Oscar Wilde. (0-486-26478-5)

FICTION

FLATLAND: A ROMANCE OF MANY DIMENSIONS, Edwin A. Abbott. (0-486-27263-X)

PRIDE AND PREJUDICE, Jane Austen. (0-486-28473-5)

CIVIL WAR SHORT STORIES AND POEMS, Edited by Bob Blaisdell. (0-486-48226-X)

THE DECAMERON: Selected Tales, Giovanni Boccaccio. Edited by Bob Blaisdell. (0-486-41113-3)

JANE EYRE, Charlotte Brontë. (0-486-42449-9)

WUTHERING HEIGHTS, Emily Brontë. (0-486-29256-8)

THE THIRTY-NINE STEPS, John Buchan. (0-486-28201-5)

ALICE'S ADVENTURES IN WONDERLAND, Lewis Carroll. (0-486-27543-4)

MY ÁNTONIA, Willa Cather. (0-486-28240-6)

THE AWAKENING, Kate Chopin. (0-486-27786-0)

HEART OF DARKNESS, Joseph Conrad. (0-486-26464-5)

LORD JIM, Joseph Conrad. (0-486-40650-4)

THE RED BADGE OF COURAGE, Stephen Crane. (0-486-26465-3)

THE WORLD'S GREATEST SHORT STORIES, Edited by James Daley. (0-486-44716-2)

A CHRISTMAS CAROL, Charles Dickens. (0-486-26865-9)

GREAT EXPECTATIONS, Charles Dickens. (0-486-41586-4)

A TALE OF TWO CITIES, Charles Dickens. (0-486-40651-2)

CRIME AND PUNISHMENT, Fyodor Dostoyevsky. Translated by Constance Garnett. (0-486-41587-2)

THE ADVENTURES OF SHERLOCK HOLMES, Sir Arthur Conan Doyle. (0-486-47491-7)

THE HOUND OF THE BASKERVILLES, Sir Arthur Conan Doyle. (0-486-28214-7)

BLAKE: PROPHET AGAINST EMPIRE, David V. Erdman. (0-486-26719-9)

WHERE ANGELS FEAR TO TREAD, E. M. Forster. (0-486-27791-7)

BEOWULF, Translated by R. K. Gordon. (0-486-27264-8)

THE RETURN OF THE NATIVE, Thomas Hardy. (0-486-43165-7)

THE SCARLET LETTER, Nathaniel Hawthorne. (0-486-28048-9)

SIDDHARTHA, Hermann Hesse. (0-486-40653-9)

THE ODYSSEY, Homer. (0-486-40654-7)

THE TURN OF THE SCREW, Henry James. (0-486-26684-2)

DUBLINERS, James Joyce. (0-486-26870-5)

FICTION

THE METAMORPHOSIS AND OTHER STORIES, Franz Kafka. (0-486-29030-1)

SONS AND LOVERS, D. H. Lawrence. (0-486-42121-X)

THE CALL OF THE WILD, Jack London. (0-486-26472-6)

SHAKESPEARE ILLUSTRATED: Art by Arthur Rackham, Edmund Dulac, Charles Robinson and Others, Selected and Edited by Jeff A. Menges. (0-486-47890-4)

GREAT AMERICAN SHORT STORIES, Edited by Paul Negri. (0-486-42119-8)

THE GOLD-BUG AND OTHER TALES, Edgar Allan Poe. (0-486-26875-6)

ANTHEM, Ayn Rand. (0-486-49277-X)

FRANKENSTEIN, Mary Shelley. (0-486-28211-2)

THE JUNGLE, Upton Sinclair. (0-486-41923-1)

THREE LIVES, Gertrude Stein. (0-486-28059-4)

THE STRANGE CASE OF DR. JEKYLL AND MR. HYDE, Robert Louis Stevenson. (0-486-26688-5)

DRACULA, Bram Stoker. (0-486-41109-5)

UNCLE TOM'S CABIN, Harriet Beecher Stowe. (0-486-44028-1)

ADVENTURES OF HUCKLEBERRY FINN, Mark Twain. (0-486-28061-6)

THE ADVENTURES OF TOM SAWYER, Mark Twain. (0-486-40077-8)

CANDIDE, Voltaire. Edited by Francois-Marie Arouet. (0-486-26689-3)

THE COUNTRY OF THE BLIND: and Other Science-Fiction Stories, H. G. Wells. Edited by Martin Gardner. (0-486-48289-8)

THE WAR OF THE WORLDS, H. G. Wells. (0-486-29506-0)

ETHAN FROME, Edith Wharton. (0-486-26690-7)

THE PICTURE OF DORIAN GRAY, Oscar Wilde. (0-486-27807-7)

MONDAY OR TUESDAY: Eight Stories, Virginia Woolf. (0-486-29453-6)

NONFICTION

POETICS, Aristotle. (0-486-29577-X)

MEDITATIONS, Marcus Aurelius. (0-486-29823-X)

THE WAY OF PERFECTION, St. Teresa of Avila. Edited and Translated by E. Allison Peers. (0-486-48451-3)

THE DEVIL'S DICTIONARY, Ambrose Bierce. (0-486-27542-6)

GREAT SPEECHES OF THE 20TH CENTURY, Edited by Bob Blaisdell. (0-486-47467-4)

THE COMMUNIST MANIFESTO AND OTHER REVOLUTIONARY WRITINGS: Marx, Marat, Paine, Mao Tse-Tung, Gandhi and Others, Edited by Bob Blaisdell. (0-486-42465-0)

INFAMOUS SPEECHES: From Robespierre to Osama bin Laden, Edited by Bob Blaisdell. (0-486-47849-1)

GREAT ENGLISH ESSAYS: From Bacon to Chesterton, Edited by Bob Blaisdell. (0-486-44082-6)

GREEK AND ROMAN ORATORY, Edited by Bob Blaisdell. (0-486-49622-8)

THE UNITED STATES CONSTITUTION: The Full Text with Supplementary Materials, Edited and with supplementary materials by Bob Blaisdell. (0-486-47166-7)

GREAT SPEECHES BY NATIVE AMERICANS, Edited by Bob Blaisdell. (0-486-41122-2)

GREAT SPEECHES BY AFRICAN AMERICANS: Frederick Douglass, Sojourner Truth, Dr. Martin Luther King, Jr., Barack Obama, and Others, Edited by James Daley. (0-486-44761-8)

GREAT SPEECHES BY AMERICAN WOMEN, Edited by James Daley. (0-486-46141-6)

HISTORY'S GREATEST SPEECHES, Edited by James Daley. (0-486-49739-9)

GREAT INAUGURAL ADDRESSES, Edited by James Daley. (0-486-44577-1)

GREAT SPEECHES ON GAY RIGHTS, Edited by James Daley. (0-486-47512-3)

ON THE ORIGIN OF SPECIES: By Means of Natural Selection, Charles Darwin. (0-486-45006-6)

NARRATIVE OF THE LIFE OF FREDERICK DOUGLASS, Frederick Douglass. (0-486-28499-9)

THE SOULS OF BLACK FOLK, W. E. B. Du Bois. (0-486-28041-1)

NATURE AND OTHER ESSAYS, Ralph Waldo Emerson. (0-486-46947-6)

SELF-RELIANCE AND OTHER ESSAYS, Ralph Waldo Emerson. (0-486-27790-9)

THE LIFE OF OLAUDAH EQUIANO, Olaudah Equiano. (0-486-40661-X)

WIT AND WISDOM FROM POOR RICHARD'S ALMANACK, Benjamin Franklin. (0-486-40891-4)

THE AUTOBIOGRAPHY OF BENJAMIN FRANKLIN, Benjamin Franklin. (0-486-29073-5)

NONFICTION

THE DECLARATION OF INDEPENDENCE AND OTHER GREAT DOCUMENTS OF AMERICAN HISTORY: 1775-1865, Edited by John Grafton. (0-486-41124-9)

INCIDENTS IN THE LIFE OF A SLAVE GIRL, Harriet Jacobs. (0-486-41931-2)

GREAT SPEECHES, Abraham Lincoln. (0-486-26872-1)

THE WIT AND WISDOM OF ABRAHAM LINCOLN: A Book of Quotations, Abraham Lincoln. Edited by Bob Blaisdell. (0-486-44097-4)

THE SECOND TREATISE OF GOVERNMENT AND A LETTER CONCERNING TOLERATION, John Locke. (0-486-42464-2)

THE PRINCE, Niccolò Machiavelli. (0-486-27274-5)

MICHEL DE MONTAIGNE: Selected Essays, Michel de Montaigne. Translated by Charles Cotton. Edited by William Carew Hazlitt. (0-486-48603-6)

UTOPIA, Sir Thomas More. (0-486-29583-4)

BEYOND GOOD AND EVIL: Prelude to a Philosophy of the Future, Friedrich Nietzsche. (0-486-29868-X)

TWELVE YEARS A SLAVE, Solomon Northup. (0-486-78962-4)

COMMON SENSE, Thomas Paine. (0-486-29602-4)

BOOK OF AFRICAN-AMERICAN QUOTATIONS, Edited by Joslyn Pine. (0-486-47589-1)

THE TRIAL AND DEATH OF SOCRATES: Four Dialogues, Plato. (0-486-27066-1)

THE REPUBLIC, Plato. (0-486-41121-4)

SIX GREAT DIALOGUES: Apology, Crito, Phaedo, Phaedrus, Symposium, The Republic, Plato. Translated by Benjamin Jowett. (0-486-45465-7)

WOMEN'S WIT AND WISDOM: A Book of Quotations, Edited by Susan L. Rattiner. (0-486-41123-0)

GREAT SPEECHES, Franklin Delano Roosevelt. (0-486-40894-9)

THE CONFESSIONS OF ST. AUGUSTINE, St. Augustine. (0-486-42466-9)

A MODEST PROPOSAL AND OTHER SATIRICAL WORKS, Jonathan Swift. (0-486-28759-9)

THE IMITATION OF CHRIST, Thomas à Kempis. Translated by Aloysius Croft and Harold Bolton. (0-486-43185-1)

CIVIL DISOBEDIENCE AND OTHER ESSAYS, Henry David Thoreau. (0-486-27563-9)

WALDEN; OR, LIFE IN THE WOODS, Henry David Thoreau. (0-486-28495-6)

NARRATIVE OF SOJOURNER TRUTH, Sojourner Truth. (0-486-29899-X)

THE WIT AND WISDOM OF MARK TWAIN: A Book of Quotations, Mark Twain. (0-486-40664-4)

UP FROM SLAVERY, Booker T. Washington. (0-486-28738-6)

A VINDICATION OF THE RIGHTS OF WOMAN, Mary Wollstonecraft. (0-486-29036-0)